THE ANGLING LETTERS OF
G. E. M. SKUES

Books by G. E. M. Skues

THE WAY OF A TROUT WITH A FLY

NYMPH FISHING FOR CHALK STREAM TROUT

and

MINOR TACTICS OF THE CHALK STREAM

THE ANGLING LETTERS OF
G. E. M. SKUES

Edited by
C. F. WALKER

LONDON
ADAM & CHARLES BLACK

FIRST PUBLISHED 1956

REPRINTED 1975

A. AND C. BLACK LTD

4, 5 AND 6 SOHO SQUARE LONDON WIV 6AD

© 1956 A. AND C. BLACK LTD

PRINTED IN GREAT BRITAIN BY
REDWOOD BURN LIMITED, TROWBRIDGE AND ESHER

CONTENTS

FOREWORD

by John D. D. Evans

Skues was a sensitive man and I think he would have been greatly displeased if many of the personal remarks in his private letters had been made public in this book. Commander Walker has been at great pains, and rightly so, to sort out from the mass of correspondence just what should be included and what should not. As one who has loaned a very large number of these letters I feel well satisfied that he had accomplished his difficult task with tact and sound judgement. I have no manner of doubt that they will be welcomed by those who survive of Skues's old friends and particularly by those who enjoyed the great privilege of spending odd week-ends at the Corner House. They will surely also be much appreciated by the many discriminating fly-fishers who know him only through his books.

Skues's writings already published and now supplemented by this compilation of a large number of his private letters, long cherished and preserved by the recipients, certainly give a fair insight into much of his character. It was, however, a most complex and sometimes rather baffling character and I am tempted by this opportunity to add some light on certain of its facets which may not show clearly either in previous writings or in these letters,

I have already described him as a sensitive man. He was also "touchy" to an extreme degree in certain matters, and he had a feeling, almost amounting to an obsession, for his beloved Itchen trout. Moreover he was as squeamish as could be imagined about some things, which was most curious in a man who frequently made the most detailed examinations of a trout's stomach contents! Here is a story illustrating both traits:

One hot and sultry July afternoon (and nearly all my visits were at this rather unpropitious season) he sent me, still carrying an empty basket, up the sidestream to search for what looked a forlorn hope. But below the weed rack, then holding vast masses of evil-smelling cut weeds, I did find a feeding trout of worthy size. This fish cruised continuously, only very occasionally stopping to take something from the surface or just below it. I tried it in vain for near an hour with nymphs and floaters. Skues then turned up and firmly refused my invitation to have a shot. While he watched, I tried the fish with various choices selected by him and finally, putting on a floating red spinner, of a pattern I didn't at all fancy and so had never used before, I at last drew its attention and it sailed out and took it.

When it was safely ashore, no time was lost. Out came the marrow scoop, which extracted a hetero-geneous mass of decaying weed, odd nymphs and caddis, the whole topped with several magnificent white maggots!

"What are those disgusting things?" said Skues, in a tone of voice reminiscent of a form master reprimanding some naughty boy at a back desk.

"Rat-tailed maggots," quoth I, "larvae of those fat brown Hover Flies you see around."

"Well, I think it is quite disgusting that *our* trout should eat such revolting things," he replied!

So genuinely upset was he that he could not remove the thought from his mind, but referred to it a dozen times that evening and the next day. Finally he said, "We must see that they clear that weed rack more often, so that the beastly things can't breed there!"

Another, probably better known, trait in his character, and one of which flashes occur at intervals throughout his writings, was a spice of impish wickedness which would suddenly crop up quite unexpectedly. The best example of this which I can recall happened on another of those hot July afternoons. This time we had each taken a fish during the morning, lunched at the Hut and then gone our ways, he down and I upstream.

Where the river runs deeper and narrower near the Poplars, forming a well defined deepish pool, I found a decent trout poised in mid-stream, at near two feet below surface. He was very much awake, turning a foot or more aside now and then to take an ascending nymph and much less often coming right to the surface to take an occasional Pale Watery dun. I plied him with all I had, nymphs and floaters, without getting the least response. Skues then turned up, remarking that he didn't look an easy one, with which I heartily agreed. Again, good host that he was, he stoutly refused my request that he should have a try at him.

After more fruitless efforts we decided that both sides should have a rest, and retired to the stile a short way downstream. We were propping up the stile and I was starting up a pipe when Skues turned to me with that curious wicked twinkle in his "good" eye and said, "Have you got any of your Usk flies with you?"

Now it so chanced that I had a few. They were in an old-fashioned leather fly-book in which I kept odd casts etc. at that time. "Let me look", says Skues, and he opened the book at the central flannel "page", so often seen carrying some motheaten relics. Here there was nothing like that. There were a few large-sized Early Olive nymphs and, *mirabile dictu*, my "best ever" effort at a single-winged wet pattern Pale Watery, securely tied to a short length of looped gut.

"That looks just what we want," he remarked. "Put it on as intended as dropper fly, and keep the nymph you have on as tail fly."

Orders were strictly obeyed and I then asked how he would like me to use this outfit. "Oh, do it your own way, just as you would on the Usk," was the answer, and I braced myself for the attack.

A careful cast, with all thoroughly wetted, brought my pair of flies over the trout without drag and so that he had a free choice of either, had he the inclination, and I remember wondering what Skues would say if the fish turned to his right and selected the chalk-stream nymph. However he did nothing of the sort, but turned left towards the Usk dropper fly and absorbed it as though it was something he really wanted!

I heard a chuckle behind me as the hooked trout dashed off, and then the quiet remark, "I knew it could be done. After all, they used to catch them that way a hundred years ago."

I never saw Skues more pleased than he was over this episode, but he remarked rather sadly afterwards what a pity it was he couldn't put it on record. The nymph controversy was then at its height and he feared that this instance of the revival of an art commonly practised a hundred years ago might add fuel to the flames.

The softening effect of time allows me now to do what Skues would have liked to do then and I welcome the opportunity. I may add that I never repeated the experiment, nor indeed have I fished the sunk winged fly in that form on my own Usk for thirty years and more, while admitting that I probably enjoyed this little episode almost as much as Skues did. I have related these two episodes here because they seem to me to serve in throwing another small beam of light on Skues's unusual and interesting character.

In this book you will find many another glimpse and I feel that many will share my deep sense of gratitude to Commander Walker for so courageously undertaking this formidable task. Had it never seen the light of day, the loss to many would have been a severe one.

I feel happy to think that here is a book which will give great pleasure and interest to many a good fly-fisher, whether he pursues the trout in the favoured chalk streams or in the rougher waters of the West and North.

EDITOR'S PREFACE

DURING the past few years it has more than once been suggested to me by friends of the late G. E. M. Skues that I should collect and edit a representative selection of his letters for publication in book form. I confess, however, that I was extremely reluctant to undertake the task, not only on account of the time and trouble involved in wading through the vast mass of correspondence believed to be in existence, but more especially because I felt—and still feel—that the Editor of such a book should be someone who had known Skues intimately. As I myself did not join the Flyfishers' Club (his habitual resort in pre-war days) until a year or so before Skues left London for good, my acquaintance with him was limited to watching from a respectful distance, as befitted a new member, while he tied his beautiful little trout flies, and to a brief correspondence some years later concerning an article which had aroused his interest in *Game and Gun*, of which I was then the Editor.

Eventually, however, as no one else came forward and I was impressed by the desirability of the work being undertaken before all Skues's friends had passed beyond human ken, I agreed to take it on. At all events, I consoled myself, I had one qualification for the task: I had read Skues's books so often that I practically know them all by heart. As time went on, moreover, I found I had another still more valuable asset. This was the (purely fortuitous) knack of being able to decipher Skues's handwriting, which grew smaller and more illegible with each succeeding year until it baffled even some of his most regular correspondents.

When it came to selecting the letters for publication my task proved much less formidable than I had anticipated. It was, in fact, almost disappointingly easy, for unhappily many of the letters known to have been preserved were not, for one reason or another, available to me. In one or two cases the recipients could not bear to part from them, even temporarily: in others they had changed their addresses and could not be traced. Saddest of all was the case of one of Skues's most prolific correspondents who took great trouble to get his desk out of store for me, only to find that all his papers, including hundreds of Skues's letters to him, had vanished. To me and to the readers of this book this is a serious loss, for many of these letters were of the very greatest interest; to their owner, it is little less than a tragedy.

At the publishers' request I have omitted all personal details from the letters chosen for publication, leaving only those paragraphs dealing with matters of practical interest to fishermen. I have also endeavoured to avoid references to incidents which have already been described in Skues's own books, though it has proved impossible not to cover much of the same general ground.

The arrangement of the letters presented several problems, but in the end I decided to group them according to subject instead of presenting them in strict chronological order, as is perhaps the more usual method. This has necessitated splitting up some of the letters and spreading them over two or more chapters, but it seemed to me that the reader would find it more convenient to pursue each subject to its conclusion than to dodge continually from one subject to another, losing the threads of each in the process.

A book of this kind demands the co-operation of a number of people, and my thanks are due to all those who so kindly responded to my requests for the loan of Skues's letters. As was only to be expected, a good many of those I received fell outside my terms of reference for one reason or another, but I hope that the owners of the letters I have been compelled to omit will appreciate my difficulty and not think me ungrateful.

In conclusion, I must express my very special thanks to Mr. C. A. M. Skues, the youngest brother of G.E.M.S., and to Major J. D. D. Evans, one of his close friends. Both of them have made a number of valuable suggestions, which I have incorporated in the book, while the patience they have shown and the trouble they have taken in answering my innumerable questions have greatly simplified my task.

C. F. WALKER

Tillington, Sussex
September, 1955

CHAPTER I

BIOGRAPHICAL

GEORGE EDWARD MACKENZIE SKUES was born on 13th August, 1858, at St Johns, Newfoundland, being the eldest child of William Mackenzie Skues, then Surgeon of the Newfoundland Companies, and his wife Margaret, daughter of Christopher Ayre, Clerk of Parliament and acting Colonial Secretary of the colony. At the age of three he was brought home in a sailing ship, and two years later, when his father was posted to India, he and his two sisters were left in the charge of their grandparents, who were then living in Somerset.

When he was five years old he saw his first trout in a tributary of the Yeo, and it made him tremble with excitement. But although he discovered more than forty years later that his grandfather had been a Don fly fisherman, there was no fishing or even talk of fishing during his Somerset days, and some twelve years were to pass before the young Skues cast his first fly over a trout.

Owing to the movements of his parents Skues attended several different schools as a small boy, and at each of them he found himself irresistibly attracted towards the nearest water. From the age of seven onwards he fished in turn for newts, wrasse, eels and bass, but his first recorded capture was an unfortunate hen, which took the bait dangling from his rod point as he was returning from an unsuccessful expedition after eels. After playing the bird for a hundred yards or so he was finally compelled to cut his horsehair line, and as he was unable to afford another this put an end to his fishing for some time.

In 1872 he sat for a scholarship examination at Winchester College—not with any idea that he might be successful, but in order to give him experience of such exams in the hope that he might later gain a scholarship to some lesser public school. To his own astonishment, however, he gained fourteenth place out of 150 candidates, and thereby became a foundation scholar of Winchester, on the banks of the river beside which, for fifty-six years, he was to spend most of his leisure time. His success also brought in sundry tips, out of which he bought a one-and-sixpenny rod, a hank of twisted silk line and some gut. With this outfit he caught many small bass in the creeks round Alverstoke, where for some years he spent his holidays, and on one memorable occasion 20 roach weighing 16lb from the Meon. But it was, of course, no use for fly fishing, and it was not until 1875 that Skues was able to acquire a fly rod and the requisite accessories, together with a licence to fish that part of the Itchen known as Old Barge and Logie Stream.

Unlike Edward Grey (afterwards Lord Grey of Fallodon), who was four years his junior, Skues met with scant success as a trout fisherman while he was at Winchester. Both suffered from quite unsuitable rods—Grey's a whippy thirteen-footer, Skues's a stiff pole of eleven feet—but Grey had the advantage of several years' wet-fly fishing on northern streams behind him when he came to the Itchen. Furthermore, he fished Old Barge for four successive summers, and was fortunate enough to meet there that great fisherman, G. S. Marryat, and to profit by his instruction in the art of dry-fly fishing. Skues, on the other hand, was only able to fish there for two seasons and had no one to set his feet on the right path. He caught the first trout of his life in July, 1875—prophetically enough on a sunk fly, although floaters had then been in common use on the Itchen for many years. This was his sole capture during the season, and in the following year he only caught three or four. In his last year, 1877, he was too busy working for an exam to have time for fishing.

In 1878 he entered the office of his family's solicitor, Mr James Powell, as articled clerk, and as he had to live in London on £80 a year, trout fishing was of course out of the question. He therefore had to content himself with fly fishing for dace and chub on the Thames until, in May 1883, Mr Irwin E. B. Cox, a client of the firm and one of the proprietors of *The Field*, invited him to fish the Abbots Barton stretch of the Itchen, between Winchester and Kingsworthy. Here he met Francis Francis, William Senior and other notable anglers, and as time went on his visits became more and more frequent until Mr Cox, seeing his enthusiasm, gave him standing leave to fish the water whenever he liked.

On the death of his parents in the early 'nineties Skues, as the eldest of the family, became responsible for the welfare of seven brothers and sisters, the two youngest of whom were still at school; a responsibility he discharged most faithfully. Towards the end of 1892, however, he himself nearly died from double pneumonia (or so he believed), but a strong constitution pulled him through, and a voyage to South Africa and back finally restored him to health. In 1894 he and his sisters moved to a house in South Croydon, then almost in the country, and in the following year he became a partner in his firm.

In these comparatively early days Skues enlarged his fishing experiences by spending holidays on the Coquet, Yore, Tweed, Teme and South Esk, as well as in Bosnia, Norway and Bavaria, but it was the chalk streams, and above all his first love, the Itchen, which attracted him most. He was therefore extremely fortunate in being able to spend his weekends on the Abbots Barton water, and here it was that he developed the theory and practice of nymph fishing with which his name will always be associated.

He continued to fish this water as the guest of Mr Cox until the latter gave up his lease in 1919, when it was taken over by a small syndicate of which Skues was one. At that time the fishery was suffering from war-time neglect, and the story of its rehabilitation has already been told by Skues himself. Although Abbots Barton, like every other water, had its up and downs, the syndicate, on the whole, enjoyed sport of a very high quality. Skues, however, was apt to take the best years at Abbots Barton as his standard and to be dissatisfied with anything less, which must in some measure have detracted from his enjoyment of fishing as a whole. But the fact is that he had been born (piscatorially speaking) with a silver spoon in his mouth, and knew little of the weariness of fishing hard-flogged hotel or association waters, which is the lot of most beginners nowadays.

For some years the syndicate seems to have been a very happy little party, but later on changes in its personnel upset the former tranquillity. First came a proposal to stock the water with stew-fed fish, then the guest days were reduced in number and finally abolished altogether. To both of these innovations Skues was strongly opposed, but was outvoted by the other rods. Finally, his colleagues made it clear that they objected to his fishing the artificial nymph, upon which Skues took the momentous decision to resign his membership. Thus it came about that in 1938, at the age of eighty, he bade farewell to the water he had fished for fifty-six years and took a rod on the Nadder near Wilton.

In 1940 family affairs made it expedient for him to leave Croydon, so he retired from his firm and took up his quarters at the Nadder Vale Hotel, on the banks of the river. Then, on the lease of the water changing hands, he once more lost his fishing. Disappointed but still undaunted, he thereupon joined a club with fishing rights on the Nadder and Wylye, although this entailed a journey by 'bus to and from the water. He continued to fish this stretch for trout in summer and grayling in the autumn until the end of the 1945 season, when increasing infirmity compelled him, at the age of eighty-seven, to lay aside his rod for ever.

After this he stayed on at the Nadder Vale Hotel until it closed down in 1948, when, after a short sojourn in Wilton, he moved to Beckenham so as to be near his youngest brother, C. A. M. Skues. There he died, quite suddenly, as the result of an internal haemorrhage, in August 1949, within a week of his ninety-first birthday. He was unmarried.

.   .   .   .

As a chalk stream fisherman Skues had few, if any, equals. Indeed, J. W. Hills, who had met most of the outstanding fishermen of his day, placed him, with one other unnamed, in a class by themselves as catchers of fish. It was his remarkable powers of observation, coupled with a logical mind which led him more often than not to the correct deductions, which raised him above the level of the ordinary first-class performer, but he was also a master of his rod and line. The Abbots Barton water is very exposed, yet a friend of his, Dr E. A. Barton, has recorded how, despite the handicap of a damaged right wrist, he would cast over a trout time after time with unfailing accuracy regardless of the strength and direction of the wind. To meet these rather exceptional conditions he had evolved, apparently without realising it, a peculiar casting technique of his own, in which the nearest part of the line hit the water first, the rest then unrolling itself on the surface, with the fly falling last of all. In effect it was something like the Spey cast, but the execution was, of course, entirely different, as it was performed in an upstream direction and with a dry as well as a wet fly.

Dr Barton, himself a first-rate chalk stream man, also noted that his friend did not always trouble to conceal himself when fishing, although the banks at Abbots Barton are bare of trees and in some places raised above the water level; yet he did not scare the fish as other anglers would have done in like circumstances. The fact is that in the course of years Skues seemed to have penetrated the very minds of the trout, until he knew exactly what liberties he could take with them.

Skues was the ideal fishing companion; unselfish, generous and sympathetic. He also possessed a delightful sense of humour and, on occasions, showed a ready wit which those who did not know him well sometimes found a trifle disconcerting. Yet his wit was never unkind, at all events at the expense of individuals. When it came to public bodies such as the Catchment Boards, for whose machinations his logical mind could find no satisfactory explanation, he did not hesitate to express his candid opinion in no uncertain terms. He also found it difficult to suffer angling fools gladly. To him, the chief delight of fishing lay in the opportunities it afforded for the exercise of observation and deduction, and he himself was always learning something fresh up to the end of his long life. The attitude of those who are content merely to accept what they read or are told, without thinking things out for themselves, was almost incomprehensible to him. As he wrote to a friend:

'I think one of the trials of fishermen who use their brains is the stupidity of the average angler. He does not want to be educated. Ivory from the ears upward.'

But perhaps what most nearly succeeded in rousing him to anger were the well-meaning people who referred to him as an authority. 'Please do not call me an authority', appears in many of his letters to correspondents who did not know him well. His attitude in the matter was not dictated by any false modesty: it was simply that, to him, the term implied finality, and in his view there was always something fresh to be learned, both by the individual and for the angling fraternity as a whole.

It is too early to attempt a precise assessment of Skues's place as an angling author, though there can be no question that his books will be read for as long as men continue to fish for trout with a fly. His first book, *Minor Tactics of the Chalk Stream*, was published in 1910 and marked the beginning of his long campaign to restore the wet fly to its rightful place on the chalk streams, from which it had been banished during the outbreak of dry-fly fever which swept through Hampshire and the adjoining counties towards the end of the nineteenth century. Although it certainly caused a sensation in chalk stream circles it was written in such modest language, and with such an entire absence of dogmatism, that even the most bigoted dry-fly purist could hardly have taken exception to it.

The Way of a Trout With a Fly, which followed in 1921, was originally intended to have been a complete treatise on the theory and practice of dressing trout flies. Eventually, however, the realisation that no one really knew what flies looked like to the trout caused Skues to abandon the project. Nevertheless, the book includes a number of original and interesting chapters on fly dressing and the author's theories on the vision of trout, in addition to a further selection of minor tactical studies arising from his experience during the eleven years which separated his first two books.

His third book, *Side-lines, Side-lights and Reflections*, followed the second after a similar interval, and consists of a somewhat miscellaneous collection of papers dealing with almost every conceivable aspect of trout fishing. Although Skues himself never cared for this book, we have reason to be grateful to those of his friends who persuaded him to collect together for the benefit of posterity all this material, of which the greater part would otherwise have remained buried in journals not available to the general public. Being much wider in scope than his other books, moreover, it enabled him to exploit to the full that rich vein of humour of which his more serious works afford but an occasional glimpse.

The last of his books to be published during his lifetime is, by contrast, more in the nature of a text-book than any of the others. *Nymph Fishing for Chalk Stream Trout* (1939) was written chiefly as a protest against the ignorance displayed both by fishermen and tackle dealers of the true art of fishing the nymph, which had given rise to a prejudice against this form of angling in certain quarters. It was his final word on the subject, and represents the outcome of a lifetime's observation and experience.

Two further books from his pen were published after his death: *Silk, Fur and Feather*, a collection of articles on fly tying which had appeared many years earlier in the *Fishing Gazette*, and *Itchen Memories*, consisting chiefly of hitherto unpublished papers relating to his experiences on the river he loved best. The latter, unfortunately, is marred by an inordinate number of errors arising from the difficulty of reading his writing, which became smaller and more illegible as he grew older.

Unlike Halford, who retired from business at the age of forty-five, Skues worked for his living until he was over eighty, and for such a busy man his literary output was prodigious. Beginning with a letter to the *Fishing Gazette* in 1888, his pen was seldom idle over a period of some sixty years. In his early days he was an inveterate theatre-goer and entertained ambitions to become a playwright, but after a few unsuccessful efforts in this direction he abandoned the idea and devoted his undoubted literary talents entirely to fishing, for which his easy, almost conversational, style was admirably suited.

When writing for the *Fishing Gazette* he used the pen-name Val Conson (the legal abbreviation for 'Valuable consideration') as a hint that some small remuneration would not be unwelcome; a hint which the Editor appears to have been very slow to take! In later years, however, when he began writing for *The Field*, William Senior, who was then Angling Editor, objected to the use of this name on the somewhat curious grounds that it only held good for his articles in the *Fishing Gazette*. For some reason he did not care to use his own name, and in casting round for a substitute he recalled that when, during his Winchester days, he had been indiscreet enough to mention that a Marquis of Seaforth figured in his ancestry, a wit had promptly dubbed him The Marquis of Seaforth and Soforth and the Isles Thereof. He thereupon took to signing his *Field* articles Seaforth and Soforth, which was later sometimes abbreviated to S.A.S.

Partly, no doubt, due to a damaged wrist, Skues became an ardent champion of light rods, and was one of the first to appreciate the possibilities of the American trout rods weighing half an ounce or so to the foot. When, in the early years of the present century, a prolonged controversy on the subject took place in the angling press he plunged wholeheartedly into the fray, and it was largely due to his influence that the heavy, wrist-breaking weapons formerly considered essential for chalk stream fishing gave place to the 5-ounce rods in general use today.

As time went on Skues found himself writing more and more frequently, not only for *The Field* and *The Fishing Gazette*, but also for smaller and more specialised publications such as *The Salmon and Trout Magazine*, *The Bulletin of the Anglers' Club of New York* and the *Journal of the Flyfishers' Club*. In the last-named he often had two articles in a single issue, so that he conceived the idea of adopting a number of different pen-names, each appropriate to the subject in hand. Thus papers containing statistical information would be signed E.O.E., and those of a humorous nature with some punning pseudonym such as B. Hinde or I. Caunter Fordham. In his tales of The Novice, in which he assumed an air of shocked rectitude, he became Integer Vitae.

Skues was never at a loss for a subject to write

about, and as he wrote for pleasure rather than profit, he never became hackneyed. Nor was he ever didactic—a fault which is all-too common amongst authors of fishing books. The lessons he had to teach were imparted gently, almost apologetically, by means of examples from his own experience at the riverside, and he must have had a wonderful memory, for he never kept an angling diary, although he made several abortive attempts to do so. For one so thorough and meticulous in all he did the omission was indeed remarkable, not to say regrettable, for what a fascinating and invaluable record it would have made.

In addition to his published writings, Skues carried on a vast correspondence with anglers all over the world. Many of his correspondents were complete strangers who, after reading his books, sought his help with their fishing problems. He became, in fact, the oracle of chalk stream fishermen, as Halford had been to those of the previous generation. To every letter, whether from friend or stranger, he replied promptly and punctiliously, and no one who sought his help or advice ever went empty away. His unfailing kindness and courtesy in this respect brought their own reward, for when at length, owing to age and infirmity, he was compelled to give up fishing and fly tying, he found much solace in his angling correspondence. Thus, at the age of eighty-nine we find him writing to a friend:

'I sat down this morning with a list of twenty-one letters, including yours, to answer. I have done six up to lunch and this is the seventh.'

He lived in comparatively good health for nearly

two years after this, and it is pleasant to think of him deriving vicarious enjoyment from the angling exploits of his friends right up to the last.

CHAPTER II

NATURAL FLIES

LIKE most thoughtful fly fishermen Skues took a keen interest in aquatic flies, though he made no claim to being an entomologist. Indeed, it was always a source of regret to his friends that, blessed as he was with exceptional powers of observation, he did not approach the subject of flies from a more scientific angle. Science in any form, however, seems to have been foreign to his nature, though he had a profound respect for those who understood such things and was always gratified when his tentative theories were later confirmed by a scientist.

Nevertheless, with such gifts and opportunities as were his, it would have been surprising if Skues had made no contribution to our knowledge of river flies, and in fact he was the first to draw attention to two species of duns found on our chalk streams. These were two of the four flies classed by Halford and Mosely as Pale Wateries, and said by them to be so alike as to make it unnecessary, for practical purposes, to distinguish between them. This, however, is only true of two of them: the two noticed by Skues are so entirely different, both from each other and from the remaining pair, that it did not occur to him to connect them with Halford's quartette.

The first of these duns was discovered by Skues in an autopsy on an Itchen trout in 1921, and was named by him the Large Blue-winged Pale Watery. It was not until two years later, however, when J. W. Dunne (author of *Sunshine and the Dry Fly*) captured some spinners of the same insect at Hungerford and sent them via Skues to Mosely, that it was identified as *Centroptilum pennulatum*.

On the Itchen it appeared only intermittently, and although Skues was on the look-out for it, he saw it on only three more occasions before he finally left that river in 1938. Subsequently he found two single specimens on the Nadder, both of them in spiders' webs on a cattle bridge.

His interest in this fly continued to the end of his life, and more than twenty years after he first found it we find him discussing it in correspondence with his entomologically-minded friends. Thus to Major J. D. D. Evans, of Ffrwdgrech, Brecon, he wrote:

29th October, 1943.

As and from a week or two before the end of September I noted on the Nadder fairly strong hatches of a largish dun which looked entirely white in flight, but I could not see it on the water nor did I succeed in catching an example or in finding one in a spider's web. So I dressed a few at a guess (here follows the dressing, which is given in a later chapter).

I had a doubt whether it could possibly be *C. pennulatum*, so dressed a pattern with a bluish hackle.

I had used neither when I met Sir Grimwood Mears for lunch in Salisbury and he produced a bottle containing in collecting fluid four undoubted *C. pennulatum*, two duns and two spinners, from the Avon at Amesbury where he said there were large hatches. A day or two later I was out on the Nadder when soon after noon a hatch of the white dun appeared and I tied on my guess imitation with the white hackle. The first four casts produced three rises including one trout. From then to 3.45 when I knocked off I rose and generally hooked every grayling to which I cast, without changing fly. Still I failed to catch a specimen of the fly and I became very intrigued as to whether it was *C. pennulatum* or not. A subsequent day when there was no hatch found the pattern neglected.

My previous experience of *C. pennulatum* dated back to June 1921. . . . It was two or three years before I again came across it and all told I only did so four times at intervals of several years, but always in the evening. It always looked like B.W.O. rise and I never put on the white fly[1] till the last. Then it was immediately wolfed. This was always in the evening, but on one occasion fishing to a nymphing fish with the white fly I got a trout in the afternoon. I remember this fish particularly because it had a severe cut along the back obviously due to a chain scythe, so it must have been after the July weed cutting.

A very intelligent keeper from the Upper Avon says the hatches of *C. pennulatum* there are in the morning about 11 a.m.

There can be no doubt:

(1) that the evening flies I met on Itchen in June and July were genuine *C. pennulatum*.

(2) that the flies Mears brought me recently caught on the Upper Avon were genuine *C. pennulatum*.

(3) that these were late September flies.

It seems rather incredible that the same insect should be an evening or dusk fly on Itchen and a morning fly on Avon and Nadder.

---

[1] This was not the white hackle fly previously referred to, but Skues's imitation of *C. pennulatum* dressed with a body of white lambs' wool and blue hackle.

Can you throw any light on the mystery?

Also can you tell me whether the white fly of Nadder is possibly *C. pennulatum* and, if not, what it is?[1]

I also want the colour of the legs of *C. pennulatum*.

Evans was, however, too busy with his wartime duties to reply to these questions at the time, and their correspondence, which had been carried on regularly for a number of years, then lapsed until the end of the war. But in the meantime Skues wrote an article on the subject of *C. pennulatum* for *The Salmon and Trout Magazine*,[2] one of his objects being to establish a universally-recognised English name for this fly. It appears from the following letter to another friend, Mr C. A. N. Wauton of Swansea, that objections had been raised to the name by which he had formerly known it:

19 August, 1944.

F. E. Sawyer, the Avon river keeper who gave Sir Grimwood Mears the two C.P.[3] spinners I mentioned is going into the C.P. question very thoroughly and may be reporting on it in *The Salmon and Trout Magazine* later. I doubt whether F. M. H[alford] ever saw a C.P., at any rate in the dun stage. This year I have only seen one sample—a very dried up spinner in a web. You make no suggestion for a name. Mosely[4] resents Blue-winged Pale Watery on the ground that pale watery applies to wings as well

---

[1] It was subsequently suggested by Mr F. E. Sawyer that the white fly might have been *Procloëon rufulum*.

[2] Subsequently included in the fourth edition of *The Way of a Trout with a Fly*.

[3] C.P. was the abbreviation commonly used by Skues when referring to this fly from now onwards.

[4] M. E. Mosely, a relative of Halford's, was then one of the leading authorities on the Ephemeroptera, and being a fisherman as well as an entomologist, his opinion naturally carried considerable weight.

as body. He thinks that anglers should be satisfied to let C.P. dun pass as B.W.O. but that will not do. The pattern which kills when B.W.O. is on is N.B.G. in a hatch of C.P.

A more cogent objection to Skues's name, Large Blue-winged Pale Watery (dun), is its unwieldy length, although this is not mentioned in his correspondence. No better name, however, has yet been forthcoming, and in his recent Angler's Entomology, J. R. Harris adopts Skues's name except that he omits 'Large', which is really unnecessary. The late H. D. Turing, who was Editor of *The Salmon and Trout Magazine* when the article was published, suggested that the fly should be known as the Greater Spurwing, but although this is sometimes used it is based on a feature which is invisible except under a microscope, and is therefore hardly likely to commend itself to practical anglers. The same objection applies to Turing's name for the other fly of the same genus, *C. luteolum*. From the following letters addressed to Mr F. E. Sawyer, the Avon keeper already referred to, it appears that Skues was not familiar with this species, which is another of the insects grouped by Halford under the name Pale Watery.

29th May, 1944.

I do not think I have ever seen *C. luteolum* unless it is so like an ordinary olive as to be indistinguishable to the unscientific eye. I am pretty sure that Mr Halford never saw *C. pennulatum*. He may have known *C. luteolum* if it is of the same size and general appearance as the other pale wateries. He classed C.P. as a pale watery and dressed them all alike.

And a little later:

5th August, 1944.

I thank you for your letter of yesterday with specimens of flies. I was under the impression that C.L. was as big as C.P. It appears to be much smaller, about the size of the other two pale wateries and somewhat difficult to distinguish. I cannot see why you say C.L. has been confused with the large pale watery. C.P. is three or four times the bulk of your spinner. *B. binoculatus*[1] I do not know.

I agree that Mr Turing's 'Spurwing' suggestion is unsatisfactory.

An angling friend lodging here, brought in a few evenings ago a large dark dun[2] *the size of C.P.* with a dirty green long cylindrical body, brown thorax and brown final segments of the body. It is quite new to me and Dr Kimmins does not seem to recognise it from the description.

Mr Sawyer made a special study of the two flies known as Spurwings, and a few years later wrote an article on the subject for *The Salmon and Trout Magazine*, which drew the following letter from Skues, then in his ninety-first year:

22nd January, 1949.

The January S. & T. Magazine only reached me today but I must write to congratulate you sincerely on your admirable article on the Spurwings. It is a tragedy that Mr Mosely died before its publication. For years I have maintained that by no means all the species of natural insects have been identified and recorded. Have you compared your observa-

---

[1] Another of Halford's Pale Wateries, now known as *Baëtis bioculatus*.
[2] Mr Sawyer suggests that this was *Cloëon dipterum*.

tions with those of the Swiss naturalist?[1] Sir Grimwood Mears will be pleased. Sorry I am out of the game.

The second fly to which Skues drew attention was called by him the July dun; not a very happy choice of name, as it might well lead to confusion with the July dun of Ronalds, which was probably the female of what is now called the Blue-winged Olive. Nor, for that matter, is the appearance of Skues's fly by any means confined to the month of July, Curiously enough, however, although the insect was evidently well known to him for some years before the publication, in 1921, of *The Way of a Trout With a Fly*, it was not until 1937 that he saw those spring hatches of it which are quite common elsewhere on the Itchen. In a letter to Wauton he described the experience:

20th April, 1937.

I was down on the Itchen on the 3rd and 4th April, and again last week-end.

On the 3rd April there was a pretty strong rise of a little dark dun, body very much the colour of the lead in a lead pencil and about the size of a small pale watery. In addition there were on the water a few of the pale watery and the large dark spring dun which used to be known as the February Flapper.

On the following day the February Flapper alone was in evidence.

On each day of the last week-end there were swarms of the tiny little dun of the dark body, and also of a paler dun. The dark dun seemed to me exactly like what I have been in the habit of calling the July dun, because it is the dark dun which generally appears in July; but I cannot recognise it

[1] F. J. Pictet.

in anything described in Mosely's book, or in your own. If it were my July dun appearing in April, it was a bit abnormal as regards season. I cannot recall having seen it before in April.

A week later, in reply to an enquiry from Wauton, he added the following notes to his description of the fly:

27th April, 1937.
The little dark-bodied dun had wings of the normal colour of a small dark dun, two setae, but I cannot speak of the neuration of the wings.

Strangely enough, although the artificial July dun was a favourite with Skues, he does not seem to have taken the same interest in its natural counterpart as he did in the case of *C. pennulatum*, and there is no evidence that he attempted to establish its true identity until the last year of his life, when he referred to it in a letter on flies in general to Sawyer.

8th February, 1949.
What is the scientific name of the July dun? My pattern was very deadly when the natural fly was on. Also my nymph of the same fly.

His correspondent, however, was unable to supply the answer, although he was well acquainted with the dun and its nymph. It was not until three years after Skues's death that the problem was solved by Prof. J. R. Harris in his admirable book, *An Angler's Entomology*. There he identifies it with *Baëtis scambus*, the fourth of Halford's so-called Pale Wateries, though how the latter came to group such a dark fly with three very pale ones remains a mystery. As it is, in effect, a miniature edition of the Large Dark Olive, Prof. Harris's suggestion that in future it should be known as the Small Dark Olive is an eminently sensible one. Yet although Skues never knew the identity of the fly he had, in a sense, discovered, many amateur fly-dressers must be indebted to him for his imitations of it in both the dun and nymph stages, which appeared in his first two books.

The very small Ephemeropterans of the genus *Caenis* are exceedingly difficult to imitate on account of their size. Yet they sometimes hatch out in large numbers and when they do so are eagerly devoured by the trout, wherefore they automatically qualified for the attention of Skues. Thus, to Evans he wrote:

17th September, 1936.

I just (and only just) got the last fish of my ten brace of two-pounders for the season (a 2lb. 15oz. fish) in the last minutes of my fishing. I had Sir Grimwood Mears coming to share my rod on the 29th August at 11 o'clock and his son ditto on the 30th. I had just netted the 2lb. 15oz. trout when Sir G. hove in sight and he and his son fished out my season. I had killed the fish on a 0000 midge and Sir G. hooked a larger trout—I daresay 3¼lb.—and lost it after five or six minutes' play. . . .

It occurred to me, having regard to the tiny size of the midge on which I got the last trout, to think about *Caenis*. I have at times of a summer evening found fish taking something minute with a queer sort of wiggling rise, and I have found them un-catchable. It struck me lately that perhaps they were taking *Caenis* nymph. Only one of the four kinds of *Caenis* is big enough to imitate (*C. halterata*). Mosely told me that there was a specimen in his cabinet at the British Museum (Natural History) and I went last Sunday to look at it. It is of quite sufficient size, but Mosely tells me that the specimen (which is a rich mahogany brown, going lighter at the tail) is really a greenish-yellow insect. So unless I can catch some I really don't know how to represent them. It would, however, be rather a triumph to get a basket with an imitation *Caenis* nymph on an otherwise impossible evening.

Skues does not seem to have succeeded in evolving a successful pattern of *Caenis* nymph, but his interest in these minute insects continued, as appears from the following letters to Wauton:

4th July, 1939.

During the last three week-ends on the Nadder I have been seeing a lot of an Ephemera which is new to me. It must have been a night fly as the spiders' webs were full of them in the morning. The fly was a tiny black-bodied insect of the size of a *Caenis* and with wings of the rounded *Caenis* shape. It was clearly in the spinner stage, having two long, widely divided setae. Can you tell me anything about the beast? The *Caenis* I have seen hitherto have been white with dark heads and thorax, but this insect was an entire black in the body.

6th July, 1939.

I am sure these insects must be Ephemeridae: they are exactly the shape of the *Caenis* and they have whisks, which I believe none of the Diptera have. If I can bottle you some samples next week-end I will do so. I had not attempted to check the segmentation of the body. The insects are so tiny and I have only seen them in the open air.

10th July, 1939.

As I anticipated, either because of the gale or because the season for them is over, there were no fresh little black spinners in the webs either on Friday when I arrived, or on Saturday morning or on Sunday. Nothing except dried-up insects. I collected a batch of them and enclose them in a small metal box, which I shall be glad to have back when you have done with it.

18th July, 1939.

I had noticed that some of the small, black round-winged flies that I saw during last week-end in the spiders' webs had three setae. I thought they must surely be *Caenis*. Even when they were quite fresh the bodies of some of them looked quite shiny black and I did not attribute the blackness to age or shrivel. I knew I had included some in the consignment to you that were not black-bodied because I could not disentangle them from the web without smashing them up.

12th July, 1940.

When writing to you the other day I forgot to mention that every time since I came here on 14th June that I have crossed a certain iron latticed bridge (and I cross it nearly daily) I have found the spiders' webs (which are numerous) full of dead *Caenis*, new caught, in the two forms I described to you last year, one with black thorax and white abdomen and one with thorax and abdomen both a bright shiny black. Both forms have the same type of rounded wing. It seems as though these *Caenis* forms are numerous in every web, it is rare to find an upwinged fly. The *Caenis* may be counted by dozens, but to find two or three small dark olive spinners is unusual.

A few years later Skues consulted Sawyer, who had begun to study these little flies and received from him some specimens. His reply indicates that he had, in the meantime, probably been in touch with the Natural History Museum:

27th July, 1944.

Many thanks for your letter of the 26th inst. with specimens of *Caenis*. These are the small size which swarm on the Nadder, filling every spider's web. The *Caenis* with a brownish plum-coloured abdomen is about twice the size and much rarer. I have only seen three specimens. I have ascertained that its scientific name is *C. macrura*. Kimmins says 'Common on large rivers.'

The Itchen *Caenis* which occasionally appeared in innumerable swarms was white bodied and small.

It is a great pity that Professor Harris's book was not published during the lifetime of Skues, as it contains a great deal that he would have found of absorbing interest, besides the solution to several problems which puzzled him for years. So far as the genus *Caenis* is concerned, Harris says there are four species, two with blackish bodies in the spinner stage and the other two much paler. The darker type emerge soon after dawn, which would account for Skues only finding them in spiders' webs in the mornings.

Skues often expressed the opinion that not all the British species of Ephemeroptera had been identified, and it is quite possible that he was right. During his fifty-six years on the Itchen he occasionally found duns or spinners which did not correspond with any of the species described in the books available to him, though it is possible that he might have found some of them, at least, in Prof. Harris's Entomology, had he lived to see it. A few of the flies he noticed, however, appeared only for one season, and he never saw them again; an occurrence which seems very hard to explain. This is how he summed up the matter in a letter to Evans:

19th March, 1937.

I was once indiscreet enough to suggest to Wauton that the men of science had possibly restricted unduly the number of kinds of Ephemeroptera in our rivers, and I was very properly and severely squashed. But for all that I don't feel certain. I have three times found in the Itchen flies which appeared for one season only and one of them was like a fly illustrated by Pictet as one of the Swiss Ephemeridae. One was a very brilliant olive dun with greenish wings and distinctive yellow ribs, and one was the Claret dun.[1] There were not many examples of the first, but it was seen, and not by me alone, for several week-ends, and two or three casual examples appeared several seasons later. No. 2 appeared only once, but in sheer shoals (so thick that the trout neglected them) and for one week-end only, and the Claret dun littered all the ditches with its dead and

[1] As the Claret dun (*Leptophlebia vespertina*) is found chiefly in acid waters with a peaty bottom, its appearance on a chalk stream is a matter for surprise. Major Evans, who knows the Abbots Barton water, suggests the following possible explanation. "Not far from the left bank of the river is (or was) a fair-sized lagoon, which was liable to flooding. After a long dry period the water in this lagoon, lying over a bed of sedge peat, might well become acidified, thereby creating conditions suitable for the Claret dun until the next series of floods from the river restored its alkalinity. This, of course, is no more than a guess, but it would account for the spasmodic appearance of the species."

dying bodies for two or three weeks in one season, and has never reappeared.

I dare say you have noticed that wild flowers often have violent outbreaks of efflorescence for a season and seem to exhaust their fertility for many years. I dare say some of our river insects do the same sort of thing.

On the chalk streams it is, of course, the insects belonging to the order Ephemeroptera which are of chief interest to fishermen. Consequently the references to flies of other orders are comparatively rare in Skues's correspondence. Of the 189 recognised British species of sedge-flies (Trichoptera) it is only necessary to identify one for angling purposes: the Grannom. Although this fly was formerly much commoner on the chalk streams than it is today, it never appeared on the Abbots Barton water, anyhow in Skues's time. In reply to an enquiry by Evans, however, he gave a brief account of his experiences of it on other rivers.

4th March, 1943.

My only experiences of the grannom have been on (1) the Coquet (2) the Lower Kennet (3) the Axe and (4) the Wey. The Coquet occasion was April 1889 when I knew nothing about the breeding of caddis and only learnt that a brown partridge hackle with a pea green body was good medicine when the grannom was hatching. I fished the Lower Kennet for big trout in Mayfly time in the nineties but before I found out that the L.K. trout only came to the M.F. I paid a visit to it one April (probably 1893) and found the air so full of grannom that it looked as if a horse's nose-bag full of chaff had been shaken loose in it. There were smacking sounds of sucking in the weeds due I believe to big eels feeding on grannom caddis in the case. The Axe I tried in an April not long after and found grannom strong and made successful use of partridge and green. It was several years later I found grannom at Tilford on the Wey and got out some of the weed and found it full of caddis in the pupal stage. Some years later I carried a lot of it over to the Tillingbourne and turned it in, but without much success.

My visits to the Usk were (1) to Brecon for a day and to Sennybridge for the rest of a week and (2) to Abergavenny for a length two or three miles upstream. There was no grannom hatch on either occasion. There is a grannom hatch on the Nadder but I have only had one season when I could fish before 1st May by which time the grannom is over. In 1941 there was a good grannom hatch from long swaying weed beds (Ranunculus I think) and I got several 2lb. trout. The length below on which I now have a rod does not open till 1st May.

In the circumstances you will see that my experience does not enable me to be very helpful.

It will probably surprise most south country fishermen to hear of stone-flies on the chalk streams, apart from the Willow-fly and Yellow Sally of the same order (Plecoptera), which are quite common on these rivers. In March, 1935, however, Major (now Colonel) P. M. Hammond informed Skues in a letter that he had occasionally found them both on the Kennet, near Newbury, and on the Test at Romsey. This brought the following reply:

27th March, 1935.

Apropos of the Stone Fly, I remember going down to the Kennet at Aldermaston about 1895, in April, when I found that there had been a flood which floated on to the meadows a number of pieces of rotten timber, and turning these over I found a number of large Stone Fly. That was the only occasion I ever found them there. Some years later, having tried the Stone Fly Creeper on a Norwegian river in 1900, with some success, I had some Stone Fly Creepers sent me alive from Yorkshire, and I had a Saturday afternoon on the same part of the Kennet trying to cast the Creeper upstream into likely runs between the weeds. Unfortunately the wind was rather strong downstream, and I kept flicking off my bait. Nevertheless I ran three fish, but none of them were firmly hooked.

In those days the trout averaged about 3lb. on that water, and it was rare to get one under 2lb. I had never heard of the Stone Fly being seen on the Test at Romsey. I am pretty sure they don't have it higher up.

My view of the bad flytaking habit of the Kennet fish below Newbury was not that it was wholly due to pike, but that it was largely due to there being such an enormous quantity of underwater food of much bigger size than the small fly which hatches in quantity on those waters.

The picture of Skues fishing a chalk stream with natural bait—and flicking it off into the bargain—is an entertaining one; yet the story provides a good example of his remarkable powers of observation and his readiness to experiment with unorthodox[1] methods, to say nothing of his thoroughness in providing himself with the material for his experiments in advance.

[1] Unorthodox, that is to say, on chalk streams. Creeper fishing is, of course, frequently practised on north country rivers.

CHAPTER III

ARTIFICIAL FLIES

SKUES's interest in natural flies was not, of course, purely academic: he was above all a practical fisherman, who used his powers of observation for the purpose of catching fish. To him, however, the means was of far greater importance than the end. The mere capture of a trout in itself gave him little satisfaction: he liked to feel that the fish had mistaken his artificial not only for a fly, but for the particular species of fly on which it had been feeding.

It follows, therefore, that in observing the natural insects he encountered by the riverside he was generally thinking, consciously or unconsciously, of the best means of imitating them. For he was never content with merely buying or copying the standard patterns of chalk stream flies. Nature herself, he always insisted, must be the fly dresser's model, and he was constantly experimenting with fresh imitations of the insects he found on the river or in his marrow-scoop autopsies. But although many, perhaps most, of the flies he used were of his own devising, he was quick to recognise and acknowledge the merits of useful patterns invented by others, such as the now famous Tup's Indispensable, which Skues himself named and was largely responsible for introducing to the angling public.

Skues always enjoyed having his friends down to Abbots Barton to fish with him, and in order to promote their chances of sport he often wrote to them beforehand suggesting the patterns of fly which experience had taught him would be likely to prove killing at the particular season of the year. Thus we find him writing to Evans:

1st June, 1932.

I heard yesterday from Bostock that your visit of 10th and 11th June was off and that you are coming on 23rd July. He writes this morning that he will bring you to my pub, 'The Corner House', Winchester.

Blue Winged Olive and its spinners for evening fishing of course. The Pale Watery Dun and its rusty spinner and possibly the large blue winged pale watery, which on the infrequent occasions when it appears is pretty deadly. Dressing as follows:

Hook. No. o Carlisle Round bend.

Tying Silk. Pale orange waxed with clear wax.

Hackle. Dark blue dun hen.

Body. Cream coloured lambs wool (raw as collected from the hedges in spring).

Whisks. Like hackle.

There is also a little dark dun (Pale Watery Dun size) tied thus:

Tying Silk. Pale Orange.

Hackle. Greenish olive cock.

Whisks. Greenish olive cock.

Body. Heron herl dyed olive. (Picric acid).

Wings. Dark old cock starling.

Pheasant tail in two sizes No. 1 and oo and Pale Blue Quills and Ginger Quills oo.

Iron Blue would normally be over, but the second hatch (smaller) *might* be on.

Nymphs assorted also advisable.

Our trout never take Turkey Brown or Little Yellow May dun.

The first of the two patterns here given was that devised by Skues after finding specimens of *C. pennulatum* in an autopsy in 1921, and before he knew its identity. The dressing, which despite the hen hackle seems to have been intended as an imitation of the dun, is not given in full in any of his books.[1] Curiously enough, there is no specific mention, either in his books or correspondence, of an imitation of the nymphal stage of this fly, though it seems likely that No. 13 in his final series, published in *Nymph Fishing for Chalk Stream Trout*, represents a C.P. nymph. The second pattern is, of course, his so-called July dun.

Two dressings of the small Pale Watery duns appear in his correspondence, the first of them in a letter addressed to a young friend of his, Mr D. M. Goodbody.

21st September, 1941.

I hope I am not too late to save your Itchen fishing. A letter from Barton reminded me of a September afternoon he got me years ago on the Leckford Abbas length of the Test when there was a strong hatch of that feeble little insect the autumn Little Pale Blue and between 4.30 and 7 I got five trout (none under 2lb. a level lot) weighing 10lb. 5oz. on a home-made representation tied as follows:

Hook. No. 16 B.7362.

Silk. Yellow.

Hackle. Pale blue.

Whisk. Pale blue.

Body. Yellow tying silk dubbed lightly with rabbit's poll.

Rib. Yellow tying silk unwaxed.

Wing. Pale blue from wing of black-headed gull.

The natural insect is so feeble that many, if not

---

[1] An abbreviated note of the dressing appeared in Skues's article on this fly in *The Salmon and Trout Magazine*, later republished in the fourth edition of *The Way of a Trout With a Fly*.

most, of them get blown over on their sides and are so taken by the fish. So it does not matter that the fly is not dressed to cock. Having ceased years ago to fish the Itchen in September I have not used the fly for years.

I have had, while the light lasted, three shots at reproducing the pattern, but one (of course the best) fell on the floor and though I searched hard with the aid of a powerful magnet, I failed to recover it. Here are the other two. I am sorry to say my celluloid varnish had petered out and the local chemist could not replace it, so the tying may be none too secure. If you have any and could give a dab on the heads of the flies it would make them safer.

Two of the flies were enclosed in the letter, and indeed still adorn its margin, having been carefully preserved by the recipient. The fate of the third will surely strike a sympathetic chord in the hearts of all fly dressers, though it seems almost irreverent to think of Skues, at the age of eighty-four, grovelling on the floor with a magnet in the posture so familiar so the rest of us. But the law of gravity is no respecter of persons, and Evans recalls that on one occasion he collected no less than four dozen unused flies which had fallen from the master's table! Some of them, he says, must have been there for a year or more, and were so deeply embedded in the carpet that no ordinary magnet could have shifted them.

It seems probable that the Little Pale Blue is the same fly as the Little Sky Blue of Ronalds, which Professor Harris identifies with *Centroptilum luteolum*. If so, Skues's other dressing of a small Pale Watery dun probably represents *Baëtis bioculatus*. It appears in the following letter to Mr (now Sir Tom) Eastham:

11th June, 1944.

My tie of the Pale Watery dun for the M[ay] F[ly] season is as follows:

Hook. oo Cleikum down-eyed.

Silk. Pale yellow at shoulder only.

Hackle. Pale ginger red.

Whisks. Pale ginger red.

Body. Pale yellow floss going greenish when wet.

Wings. Hen blackbird secondary doubled.

It is *very* attractive at this season to both trout and grayling.

The above pattern is, to all intents and purposes, a pale version of Greenwell's Glory.

Although Skues does not seem to have evolved a satisfactory pattern of *Caenis* nymph, he had some success with an imitation of these minute insects in the dun stage, and described the dressing in a letter to Hammond:

21st March, 1935.

I have in the past killed trout (and good trout) when *Caenis* was on thick with a fly dressed as follows:

Hook. B.7362. Size oooo.

Tying Silk. White, not waxed, but saturated with celluloid varnish.

Body. White silk untreated.

Rib. Fine silver wire.

Hackle. Pale yellow, almost white.

Wing. Young starling.

I recall one fairly recent week-end when I got with this pattern trout of 2lb. 2oz., 2lb. 5oz., and 2lb. 7oz. and a number of others under 2lb., the only one that got off being scratched. All the others were soundly hooked and came to net. This pattern of hook buries, and has at times in the small sizes to be cut out.

Skues's experience of Mayfly fishing was comparatively slight, for the Mayfly died out at Abbots Barton in his early days, and in any case it was a form of angling which had little appeal for him. Consequently he gave less attention to imitating the Mayfly than he did, at various times, to the other species of Ephemeroptera found on chalk streams, but the following letter, written in reply to a question from Eastham, suggests an original line of thought:

19th June, 1944.

I have no special M[ay] F[ly] dresssing. I do not much care for M.F. fishing. I have not had any since 1913. In that season Sir John Ward gave me two days on his wife's Chilton Foliat length of the Kennet. The first day was on the field just above Eddington Mill and I landed nineteen trout of which I kept seven weighing 19lb. I only killed the seventh because he was too hard hooked for me to extract the fly. The limit was 2lb. and I wanted to bring in a 3-pounder and I had not one of that weight among my three brace. So I went on trying and put up a special M.F. I had dressed with wings of Summer duck not curved outwards in the usual way but inwards and bound together so tight at the base that they were flat against each other and then I cut them down to the size and shape of a natural M.F. wing. At the first chuck the fly was picked off the water by a chaffinch, at the second by a swallow or martin, at the third by the same or another chaffinch, and at the fourth it was taken by a 2lb.

1oz. trout. That was hooked too hard to be put back, but the fly when extracted was ruined. I never tried any more of that special pattern because a single capture made a mess of it.

On the face of things, this would seem the most logical method of tying the wings, not only of Mayflies but of all floating patterns representing duns, since the wings of the natural insect as it floats downstream are either pressed together or only very slightly parted. One can only suppose that the V-shaped wings of the standard dry fly were originally adopted either on the supposition that they would cause the fly to drop more delicately on the water or that it would cock more certainly when it got there. If so, their originator was on the wrong track, for a hackle fly drops just as lightly as one with wings (perhaps even more so), and elsewhere Skues has stated that his 'special' Mayfly cocked perfectly on each of its four journeys. It seems a pity, then, that he did not pursue his experiments with this style of winging any further, for his ingenuity might well have found some means of overcoming the drawback he mentioned. Indeed, as there seems to be no obvious reason why his fly should have suffered any more from its immersion than an orthodox pattern, it appears more than possible that an explanation of its unusually short life is to be found in the statement that the fish was very hard hooked (i.e. presumably far back inside the mouth).

It is, of course, to Skues that we owe the discovery of the value of the Orange Quill during an evening hatch of B.W.O. duns. It is therefore somewhat surprising to find that he himself, while acknowledging the efficacy of the pattern under these conditions, was by no means convinced that it represented a dun in the eyes of the trout. This is evident from the following brief extracts from letters addressed to Evans, who had expressed the contrary view:

19th March, 1937

I have never felt quite certain of what the Orange Quill is taken for. Quite possibly you are right. One sex of the B.W.O. subimago has a certain degree of redness in the body.[1] But my impression is that the pattern is taken for a spinner.

24th March, 1937.

I, too, have often had the Orange Quill taken well when the fish were wolfing B.W.O. [duns] on the surface, but that does not seem to me conclusive proof that the Orange Quill is taken for the B.W.O. [dun]. You must have noticed often how trout will take an imitation of the spinner of a fly on the water in preference to an imitation of the fly.

31st March, 1937.

B.W.O. and Orange Quill. I don't say my suggestion is conclusive; but it makes the alternative suggestion inconclusive. Another point in favour of the spinner theory is that I have found pale starling wings on the Orange Quill more effective than darker wings, though the wing of the B.W.O. [dun] is quite a dark blue, looking almost black in the late light.

In view of Skues's strong partiality for the Orange Quill, and of the wonderful sport it brought him, it is remarkable that, even though he did not actually invent it, he never gave its dressing in any of his books. Indeed, Skues himself was evidently surprised at the omission, as appears from

[1] This is true of the male dun whose body is described by Prof. Harris as brown-orange in colour.

his correspondence with a friend, Mr A. E. N. Jordan, when his long life was drawing to its close.

30th June, 1949.

It is curious that none of my books contain the dressing of the Orange Quill, seeing that it has meant so much to me. It is winged with starling and the colour of the body is hot orange. The body is made of condor quill: it has the usual hackle and whisk.

In his chapter on the Orange Quill in *Side-Lines*, Skues described how he had searched in vain for this pattern in Halford's *Floating Flies and How to Dress Them*. Evidently, however, he had forgotten that a dressing of it was included in Halford's later volume, *Dry Fly Entomology*, a fact of which Jordan now reminded him. Skues replied as follows:

2nd August, 1949.

Your letter of 31st July reached me this morning. I have no recollection of the Orange Quill being described among the hundred best patterns.[1] I wish you would get me a copy of it.[2] I doubt it being meant for an Orange Quill. My dressing of it was discovered in 1894.

Although Skues never claimed to have invented the dressing of the Orange Quill, his first specimen of which he found in a fishing tackle shop in Winchester in the early nineties, it looks as though he was just the slightest bit nettled by this discovery that the pattern had, after all, been mentioned by Halford. At all events, his relief at Jordan's further revelations on the subject is evident from the following:

[1] i.e. in *Dry Fly Entomology*.
[2] Skues had by this time sold all his fishing library.

5th August, 1949.

Many thanks for your letter. It is very good of you to dig out Halford's Orange Quill, but it is not mine. Mine is on a number one hook and has a body of condor. Halford's was on oo or ooo hooks and he does not say what quill. It cannot be the same pattern as mine.

You have added to my information, however. Halford had a Blue-winged Olive with a dyed body of ordinary peacock quill. I am not disturbed by your discovery.

Skues had, in fact, some justification for saying that Halford's Orange Quill was not the same as his own. Apart from the fact that it was dressed on smaller hooks, Halford used peacock quill for the body, which would probably not dye such a vivid orange as condor quill. It is included in a list of eleven red or reddish spinners, but was not associated by Halford with any specific insect, least of all the B.W.O. dun.

The last of these letters was written only four days before Skues's death, so it is pleasant to think that his recollections of the Orange Quill, which had brought him so many happy and successful evenings on the Itchen, stayed with him to the last. Curiously enough, he never managed to find a floating pattern which was successful during a daytime hatch of B.W.O., when the Orange Quill is useless. He was therefore greatly interested to read in that now defunct journal, *Game and Gun*, an account of two dressings of this fly which had proved successful in daytime on a tributary of the Tweed. He at once wrote to the Editor, Commander C. F. Walker, to express his interest:

September, 1946.

May I congratulate your contributor, S.H.L., on

his having evolved dressings of the Blue-winged Olive which will take trout rising to that fly during the day time. I am in my eighty-ninth year and my hands have become too shaky for fly dressing and my fishing days are over, so that I cannot put the dressings to the test. The only pattern of B.W.O. with which I ever had any success during the day time was an imitation of the nymph tied with two shades of olive seal's fur to represent the thorax and abdomen respectively.

If S.H.L.'s B.W.O. patterns prove to be permanently successful for day time takers of B.W.O. he will have done the trout fishing community yeoman's service.

Although Skues was primarily, and in his later years exclusively, a chalk stream fisherman, he always took a lively interest in flies found on other types of rivers and the methods of imitating them. The nymph of the March Brown, in particular, attracted his attention, and led to a long correspondence with his friends Evans and Wauton, who fished in Wales, where these insects abound. The following are extracts from letters addressed to the former:

16th February, 1932.
My most successful M[arch] B[rown] nymph was dressed with a round pudding of hare's ear and the shortest brown partridge hackle I could contrive. The *Ecdyurus*[1] nymph is very broad, though flat, and if you give the fish a round pudding of a body (tapered very fast), it will look to the fish as if he

---

[1] The March Brown was formerly identified with *Ecdyurus venosus*, now known as *Ecdyonurus venosus*, the false, or late March Brown. The true M.B. is *Rhithrogena haarupi*.

were seeing it with the broad side towards him. At least that was my theory. But it is years since I attempted to fish an M.B. I am keeping your olive nymphs and return your M.B. with thanks.

2nd March, 1932.

Apropos of your M.B. nymph dressing, I wonder whether it would be possible to get some black Tup —or even some black lamb's wool. It would not be really black, but a deep rusty brown, and teased up well with hare's ear of appropriate colour would make a dubbing which could be worked into a fat short taper so as to imitate the shape of the *Ecdyurus* nymph. Apparently *haarupi* is not so tubby.

7th March, 1932.

Thanks for trying to get some black Tup. In default of Tup I daresay black lamb's wool, not necessarily from that part, might do better than nothing. A man I once knew (long since dead) named Reffitt, a Yorkshire angler, used to dye rabbits poll lightly in a sort of red ant dye and spin it on hot orange silk for March Browns. Hackled with snipe rump it is very effective. You will find the pattern described in Edmonds and Lee's *Brook and River Trouting*. They got the pattern from me. I tied a lot for a man who used to fish in Devon and he found them deadly.

9th March, 1932.

When you looked at the black lambs, did you have them turned over and look at the under fur? I am sure I have seen fur of black sheep which has a distinct rusty red in it when held to the light.

Yes, you did tell me that what you considered probably *haarupi*[1] nymph is a dark sepia colour. You did not mention that his tracheae were quite pale.

My acquaintance with the Yorkshire angler whose name was Reffitt dated back to the very early nineties. I was on the Coquet in April a good many years ago (I think about 1922) with McCaskie, and the trout that we got were full of a ruddy nymph, the colour of which would be very closely represented by that of the body of those patterns I sent you when wet.

12th March, 1932.

No doubt the ruddy nymphs of Northumberland (not Yorkshire) which I mentioned to you are the same type as the largest that you sent, but they were nothing like as big and they looked to me more purple red. Both March Browns and the dun nymphs look to me infinitely more difficult to represent than the small ones we get on the chalk streams.

His correspondence with Wauton on the subject of March Browns began five years later, and was started by a request for some nymphs tied by him.

4th March, 1937.

I wish I had a model nymph or, better still, a natural one to dress from, but I will have a shot to fill your bill on Sunday. Some years ago I spent a

---

[1] Evans later confirmed the identity of this nymph.

few days on the Coquet. There were strong hatches
of M.B., but I did not see one taken on the surface,
but the trout were full up to the back teeth of purple
hued M.B. nymphs. I dressed a pattern with pheasant tail body, hare's ear thorax and short brown
partridge hackle which McCaskie, Chaytor and
others have said to be first-rate. I will send you a
pattern with the hot orange nymphs you ask for.

Some years back Jack Evans sent me a phial with
some huge yellow dun nymphs[1] (twice the size of
the Itchen nymphs) and some odd-looking M.B.
nymphs,[2] a ruddy brown on the upper side but a
bright greenish yellow on the underside and in the
joints. It struck me as quite impossible to imitate.
They were quite flat. I imagine one of those types
was one of Mosely's M.B.s and the other the other,
but I don't know which was which. The Coquetdale
fly was a mid-April hatch and hatched in flushes,
very thick.

8th March, 1937.
I did not till Sunday last feel equal to tackling
my undertaking to tie you some big ruddy nymphs
of the M.B. class, for I have been having the vilest
cold I have sampled for years.

You asked for the nymphs to be two sizes larger
than the sponge nymphs, but as their sizes were two
and three I have done and enclose two each of four
and five. I hope I have rightly interpreted what you
wanted: but if not, tell me what is wrong and let me
have another shot.

[1] *Rhithrogena semi-colorata.*
[2] *Ecdyonurus venosus.*

As I had my vice set up and my materials out I also tied (on a No. 4) and enclose an example of the pheasant tail pattern I spoke of. Then, seeing an envelope containing a mixture of the sweepings of a series of yellow, green, olive, orange and other miscellaneous seal's furs which had been teased up together with some hare's poll to make it bind, and remembering that Norris had given me the recipe for it in the early nineties as making a good M.B. body for the Teme, I tied and enclose a sample of that. I hope that among them you will find something of use.

There is a M.B. pattern which I have never myself used but which I have tied for other anglers, and I shall be pleased to tie for you if you would like a pattern or two. I got it many years ago from a Yorkshire angler named Reffitt, who swore by it.

There was a member of the Club for whom I tied six on 2x gut to fish the Axe and he cursed me freely because he had left the whole half-dozen in trout in the first stickle. (What a wrist!)

[Then follows the dressing, which has already been given in a letter to Evans.]

I believe the mobility of the hackle is the attraction and that the trout take it for the M.B. tumbled over with wings wetted in its attempts to hatch.

9th March, 1937.

I had intended to go up to my office yesterday, but in view of the weather I thought it more prudent to keep under cover. So after I had dismissed my typist who came down to take my letters

I tied a couple of that snipe rump M.B. I described in my last letter, and enclose them. Just take the hook in your hand and blow on the hackle, and see how mobile it is. According to my recollection the snipe rump M.B.s I tied for Edmonds were ruddier in the body than these, but the dubbing of these exactly matches the material supplied to me by Reffitt years ago, and no doubt when it is wet the hot orange silk will show through the dubbing.

In his early days on the Coquet Skues had also evolved a dressing to represent the August dun, *Ecdyonurus dispar*, which he described in a letter to Evans:

21st December, 1938.

With regard to the August or Autumn dun. I do not recall ever having seen it called the Autumn dun, though I recognise the strength of the case for so naming it. In my flyfishing experience I only came across it in one period, viz.: ten days in September 1888 when I found it daily in the Coquet at Weldon Bridge. I had only begun fly-dressing in 1887 and I started to dress representations from the natural insect without any idea of what it was called. My dressing was, according to my recollection, as follows:

Hook. No. 2.
Silk. Yellow.
Body. Some pale bluish brown fur (maybe fox).
Rib. Yellow silk.
Hackle. Pale cinnamon.
Whisks. Pale cinnamon.
Wing. The bluest part of a landrail primary.

Anyhow, the trout took it, better than the commercial pattern dressed according to Ronalds.

I also successfully imitated the spinner of the August dun with flat gut dyed bright orange wound on a bare hook. It killed well in the evenings when I saw the spinners like red-hot needles dancing in the dying sunset.

So far as imitations of the Trichoptera were concerned, Skues seems to have been content, for the most part, with his own pattern of Little Red Sedge, the dressing of which he gave in *The Way of a Trout With a Fly*. In reply to a request from Eastham, however, he supplied a dressing of the Grannom which he had used with success in his earlier days:

11th April, 1945.

The grannom has no nymph. It belongs to the Sedges and the pupa emerges from its caddis case and comes to the surface to hatch, after which it flies straight away. The trout's opportunity to take it is while it swims to the surface, so winged patterns are not much good.

A useful wet pattern is dressed thus:

Hook. No. 3 round or sneck bend, down-eyed.
Silk. Green (waxed with colourless wax).
Hackle. Brown partridge.
Body. Bright green lamb's wool.

Although Skues had comparatively little experience of fishing except on the chalk streams, such was his reputation as a tyer of killing patterns that his advice was not infrequently sought regarding flies for other types of rivers. And so well did he come to understand the ways of trout that he was usually able to make a shrewd guess at the types of dressings which would prove effective under conditions of which he had no personal knowledge. Thus we find him writing to Mr S. Roberts, of Exeter:

7th February, 1945.

The flies I tied for my friend Col. Jesse to use on the little Devonshire Avon were all rather large, being on No. 2 Carlisle round bend down-eyed pattern [hook] and comprised the following:

1. Lightish dun cock's hackle and whisks.
   Body hare's poll.
2. Rusty blue cock's hackle and whisks.
   Body crimson seal's fur.
   Rib gold wire.
3. Rusty blue cock's hackle and whisks.
   Body 3 strands of pheasant tail.
   Rib gold wire.
4. Tup's Indispensable.

For that water he never seemed to want any others. I tied them as a guess as likely to suit that tumbling water and he did well with them all, particularly No. 1.

The dressings of the nymph patterns for chalk stream fishing which Skues evolved from time to time are given in his books, but occasionally he received a request for nymphs of a more unorthodox type. The following amusing reply to a *cri de coeur* from Norway is a typical example of his prompt and generous response to a friend in need. It is addressed to Mr (now Captain, R.N.V.R.) C. F. Struben, who was on a fishing holiday in that country.

11th July, 1932.

I received a cable this morning in the following terms:

'Help us fish sticky apparently nymphing taking occasional alder we can hares ear send through carter or your man airmail caple dozen suitable inducements—Struben Forsmark Slussfors.'

You must forgive me if I find it absolutely incomprehensible. I do not know what fish you are speaking of, though I imagined you had gone over for salmon fishing and not for trout.

I do not know how you 'can hares ear', nor do I know what the word 'caple' means, and even if I knew I doubt whether I could help you as my experience of Norwegian fishing is very limited.

P.S. [Written on the following morning.]

I had to send back your cable to be interpreted and the interpretation had not arrived when I left [my office] last night. I spent an hour tying the enclosed half-dozen nymphs (1st lot). They are no doubt bigger than the natural nymphs, but my small experience of Norwegian trout suggests that a big mouthful attracts them more than a small one, and that a heron herl body dyed olive (in picric acid) is not objectionable to them.

You will see that I have used a variety of hackles, experimentally. You could not buy these nymphs at any dealers. I don't know any dresser who could supply you promptly. They would take days to get the materials together.

I also rose early this morning and in my pyjamas tied you the other five nymphs of varying types (2nd lot). I enclose them to go on with, and hope they may be of some use.

The explanation of the cable is 'Wickham' for
'we can' and 'couple' for 'caple'. (Why not two?)
I take it that you are getting an occasional fish with
Alder, Hare's Ear and Wickham.

CHAPTER IV

FLY DRESSING

SKUES first began to tie his own flies in 1887 and continued to do so until 1945, when, at the age of eighty-seven, his hands became too shaky for the delicate operations involved. Those, by the way, who suffer from the not uncommon delusion that only people specially favoured by Nature with neat fingers and artistic hands are capable of tying flies, may take comfort from the example of Skues.

He could tie flies, moreover, under conditions which would utterly defeat the majority of present-day fly dressers, who need a solid bench, a fixed vice and a whole cabinet of tools and materials for their operations. Not infrequently, for instance, with a sublime disregard of his fellow-passengers, he would tie a small stock of patterns for immediate use in the train between Waterloo and Winchester. Readers of *The Way of a Trout With a Fly* will remember his delightful account of 'A travelling companion', in the shape of a live sherry spinner which he found on the window of his railway carriage one July day. By the time the train reached Farnborough he had produced three imitations of the fly, on one of which he landed a two-pounder that same evening and on another lost a much larger fish due to the hook straightening out. He was also in the habit of tying flies in his hotel before breakfast, and often his week-end fishing guest would come downstairs in the morning to find him putting away his materials after producing a small stock of patterns which experience and observation had taught him would be likely to be of service during the day.

Although Skues was always ready to experiment with new kinds of materials for fly dressing, in the end, as he wrote of nineteenth century fly dressers, he invariably came back to silk, fur and feather. Of these, as might be expected, he was a connoisseur, more especially in the matter of hackles. Even in his early days it was not easy to procure these of a quality to satisfy his critical eye, and when he had a rod on the Tillingbourne before the 1914-18 war he kept a pen of gamecocks at Chilworth. Curiously enough, he does not seem to have mentioned this in any of his books, but in a note to Evans many years later he tells of the sad fate of his cherished birds.

13th March, 1947.

Graham Clarke[1] bred his own hackles. I started my lot with a few of his birds. When I gave up I had some birds with lovely necks, and the keeper to whom I gave them promptly killed the lot and replaced them with White Dorkings and Rhode Island Reds. It was infuriating.

Later, Evans himself began to breed gamecocks for their hackles, and from time to time sent samples to Skues for his comments, a selection from which are given below.

29th July, 1932.

Many thanks for your letter of the 28th, with the hackles enclosed. The ginger hackles among them look quite nice, having a sort of honey dun tinge. The white are well enough, but not of special

[1] A well-known amateur fly-dresser in his day (1841-1920).

interest, but I should be inclined to keep the bird for another year to see whether this next crop of feathers may not be more satisfactory as regards colour.

2nd August, 1932.

It is a pity that you killed the ginger bird with blue body and ginger neck. He might have fathered some lovely honey dun chicks. I don't use dyed hackles except a few olives. I loathe whites dyed blue.

20th April, 1933.

'Shaft' is, no doubt, a much more correct word for the stem of the feather than stalk. I think you have been taking up the breeding of game fowls very much more systematically than I did. I am afraid I was rather a 'chuck and chance it' character, though I did get some not bad results. That specimen feather you sent me is quite a nice colour and has some spring in it, but I should not call it a badger. It is not either white enough or yellow enough, but is sandy or rusty. I hope you and Henderson will make a good job of it and spread the breeding of fowls for hackles for all you are worth.

6th June, 1933.

Many thanks for your letter of the 3rd, which I found awaiting me on my return from Winchester. Thanks also for the spade feathers. With one exception one would never suspect that they were from a light blue bird, as they are a deep blood red. They will make admirable whisks for floaters, though I generally use them paler except for Gold Ribbed

Hare's Ear. For some time past I have dressed Iron
Blue with a very pale blue hackle, rather staring, so
as to make the fly float cocked.

19th July, 1933.

I like the colour of the rusty dun feather that you
send me; but, being only from a yearling bird, it is,
of course, rather tender and slight, but a two-year
old, or a three-year old, ought to produce a very
fine class of feather, just the colour I like for rusty
dun and for dark pheasant tail, though sometimes a
redder feather does better for the pheasant tail. I
agree with you in liking a pronounced freckle, and
that the fish prefer them.

21st July, 1933.

That is a very nice black-red hackle that you sent
me. Although black-red hackles in themselves are
not of any great value, unless they are genuine
cochybondhu, it might very well prove a good bird
to breed from.

Did I ever tell you of a letter I saw during the
war from a man who used to breed poultry for
hackles before he went out to the front? His principle was to keep the birds he mated in separate
pens and weed out those whose colours did not
prove satisfactory, and turn them into a general
barn-yard, where, by reason of the fighting strain
in them, they monopolised the hens, and he used to
obtain, he said, wonderful crosses of all sorts of
colours. I have often thought that if I were retired
and a well-to-do man that is the sort of game I
should like to play.

I do not know what the effect of caponising is on hackles. I think I told you that a few years ago I found that the year was producing a remarkable quantity of magnificent cock's hackles, beautiful in shape and condition, and I wrote to that effect in *The Field*, the letter appearing sometime in March. I got a request from somebody to get him some of these hackles. I went again to Leadenhall Market and found all the hackles in the poorest and slimiest condition. One of the salesmen explained to me that it was because the birds that were then coming in were incubator birds, and that the previous birds had been naturally hatched.

27th July, 1933.

With regard to the hackle that you sent me it really is, to my mind, a very beautiful hackle, and honestly I question whether it is pure Andalusian. It has got so much pluck and character in it that I should think it must have a strain of game. The chalkiness at the back does exist, but it is not very pronounced.

If I had the bird I should be inclined to keep it and turn it loose in just such a general farmyard as that which I described in a recent letter. Failing putting him to run in a general yard I should certainly put him out to walk for a year, plucking him now and having his neck and skin next year. I could, by the way, do with half a dozen of the woolly sort of breast feathers, woolly pretty near the tip of each feather.

1st August, 1933.

It is rather a tragedy that the general farmyard with its mixed breeds of fowls is gone. There used

when I came to Croydon forty years ago to be
several within a Sunday afternoon's walk which I
used to visit from time to time to see the birds suitable for fly dressing. There were some blues, but
not many; more honey duns. Now there is nothing
but whites and Rhode Island Reds.

I went the year before last to a Poultry Show at
the Crystal Palace, and I saw a lot of those large
speckled grey fowls of American origin (Plymouth
Rocks) both from this country and from America. I
was amazed to see what splendid stately birds the
American fowls were. Ours seemed gross and peasant
stock by the side of them.

There were also a lot of Americans (also called
Plymouth Rocks) which were a lovely pale ginger
with no freckle in them and hackles of fine shape. I
wonder whether the Americans are attempting anything in the way of breeding fowls for fly dressing.

Have you, by the way, a spare pinch of hare's poll
—the pale pinky patch between the ears? I have let
myself run right out of it.

Being worried by the increasing difficulties of obtaining
hackles suitable for fly dressing, Skues welcomed an idea
put forward by Evans for compiling a register of those
who bred fowls for their hackles:

7th January, 1932.

You might give me the names and addresses of
any hackle breeders you know. I think the [Fly-
fishers'] Club might keep a list in two sections.
(1) amateur, (2) professional, and it might do no
harm to have a third to include those who do not
breed but supply [hackles].

I think it would be a good move for a letter to be sent to the F[ishing] G[azette], and perhaps to *The Field*, inviting professionals who breed for sale of birds and hackles to send their names for the second list, and inviting dealers in hackles and material to send their names and addresses for the third list, and inviting amateur anglers who desired or were willing to correspond for mutual assistance to send their names and addresses for the first list, and stating that members of the F[ly] F[ishers'] C[lub] might have copies of all these lists, and all non-members who sent their names might have copies of the second and third lists. Of course it would have to be done through the Secretary, and with the approval of the Committee. I expect there would be a rush of applicants to be included in lists two and three, and we might dig up some shy birds for list one who might be tempted to become members.

Skues evidently lost no time in putting his idea into practice, for a week later he wrote:

15th January, 1932.
I am glad to be able to report to you that the Committee of the F.F.C. have arranged that the Secretary shall write a letter to the [Club] Journal, to the *Fishing Gazette* and to *The Field* inviting members and non-members who are breeders of poultry for fly dressing to communicate their names and addresses, and those of any others interested to the Secretary with a view to lists being made and supplied to those who are interested.

There are to be three lists, one of members and amateurs who are non-members, another of professional breeders and another of tackle dealers and others who supply hackles.

The letters were duly written, and a list of sorts compiled, but the scheme did not meet with the support for which Skues had hoped, and nothing of value resulted from it.

Of body materials Skues's favourite was dubbing; dyed seal's fur for spinner patterns and, as a rule, soft fur for nymphs. For duns, however, he often used heron herl, which in its various shades dyed in picric acid or undyed, can be used to represent the bodies of most of the Ephemeroptera found on chalk streams. Silk bodies figure in a few of his dressings, but quill he avoided as a rule, the exceptions being the Orange Quill and two of his Medium Olive nymph dressings. In one of his earliest surviving letters, addressed to a friend of his named Edwards, he refers to the subject thus:

5th August 1919.

Yes, paraffin does darken the bodies of flies unless they are tied with seal's fur like the enclosed red spinner or quill. I confess I am not enamoured of quill bodies. I prefer herls or dubbing any day. . . .

I am sure mucilin will darken most patterns, except bodies of seal's fur, pig's wool, mohair, horsehair, gut and quill. Is the colour of the enclosed fly right for your scarlet bodied red spinner? It is meant to imitate the spinner of the August Dun, which looks like a red hot needle dancing in the sunlight. Most of the red spinners are a deep rusty red like the herl of the centre feather of the tail of a cock pheasant. That makes an excellent spinner. I have killed a lot of fish with it up to 2lb. 9oz.

At one time he experimented with rubber as a body material for dry flies, but soon gave it up for reasons expressed in a letter to Evans:

16th August, 1933.

Until recently I never saw any rubber which seemed to me to suggest the colour together with the translucency of the natural insects, but I was tempted to try the white rubber bodies for pale watery nymphs and found them not unattractive.

As a body material, however, rubber has one serious defect. It seems inclined to deliquesce. I had the misfortune to drop my nymph box in a wet place last week-end and got it pretty thoroughly soaked and I had to take out everything in it, and in the course of doing so, to condemn a large number of nymphs mainly because the gold or silver wire ribbing had tarnished, but a number of the rubber bodies also had to go because of this deliquescence.

For the bodies of most of the nymph patterns in his final series Skues used fur dubbing, but he had experimented with several other materials at various times, especially in imitating the flat-bodied nymphs of the genera *Ecdyonurus* and *Rhithrogena*, which are found chiefly on fast, rocky rivers. To Evans, who sent him a specimen nymph of the Yellow Upright (*Rhithrogena semicolorata*), he put forward the following suggestions:

29th March, 1932.

I was much struck by the branchiae on your large pale *Rhithro*. nymph. It occurs to me that you might suggest them rather well by dyeing pale Condor unstripped quill a light greenish yellow, tying in a strand by the stout end and winding it so as to have the furry edge at intervals along the nymph body. I have got similar effects with dyed peacock's brown wing feathers using single strands for the body.

2nd April, 1932.
Here is a shot at a nymph with branchiae. They are not quite long enough nor mobile enough. I dressed it by electric light so the colours are all wrong, but you see the idea. The hackle is also too long in the fibre.

6th April, 1932.
I noticed that the branchiae of your *Rhithrogena* nymphs were enormous. What I think you want is rather a longer herl than a wider nymph, but I do not know any feather with such a herl. I met a man a few days back who was keen on nymphs and tried to suggest branchiae by using the furry point of a feather spun on the tying silk. It was clever, but it is not wide enough to suggest *Rhithrogena*.

Another body material he tried was sponge, which has obvious advantages for an artificial nymph, which is required to sink as rapidly as possible. Writing of the idea to Wauton, he said:

15th February, 1937.
I have a sponge which is fast coming to pieces, and on Sunday I tied four nymph patterns with bodies of sponge and gold wire ribs. They ought to take up water freely and sink nicely. Curiously enough this is an idea I put to old George Holland (the Winchester fly dresser) as long ago as 1888, but

neither he nor I made use of the idea. The nymphs look quite attractive, and amadou will dry them thoroughly.

From the letter of 4th March in the same year, quoted in the last chapter, it is evident that he sent some samples of the sponge nymphs to Wauton, but after that there is no further mention of them, so it appears that he did not pursue the idea. Quite possibly a sponge body would prove too vulnerable to the teeth of a trout to be a practical proposition.

Skues held strong views on hooks, and whenever he gave the dressing of one of his flies, either in a letter or in his books, he always included not only the size but also the pattern of hook to be used. In the letter to Edwards, previously quoted, he stated that he never used eyed hooks for wet flies. This, however, was written in 1919, and applied to the winged wet flies he then used on the Itchen. For his imitations of nymphs, which were not fully developed until later, he used eyed hooks, as appears from a letter on the subject to Eastham:

29th July, 1944.

Yes, I use down eyed hooks for nymphs and latterly for all purposes, but that may be due to my incompetence[1] to cut away the waste roots of the feathers used for wings on an upturned eye unless I tie the wings forward with the roots of the feather back over the shaft.

If they were still to be had in the old pre-1914 quality I would only use B7362 for all sizes up to 0, but they are no longer made. For small flies I now use Pennell Snecks and Cleikum and for large flies, No. 1 up, I use Carlisle down eyed round bends.

[1] By this time Skues was close on eighty-six, and his hands were getting so shaky that soon afterwards he was compelled to give up fly-tying altogether.

Cleikum has a crank shaft so that wings tied forward sit up better than on a straight shank. The largest size made is No. 1. It is a good holder and hooker.

Fond as he was of experimenting with colour, Skues as a rule followed the strictly orthodox path when it came to form. It therefore comes as something of a surprise to find him tying Variants, especially as there is no reference to this type of fly in any of his books. The first reference occurs in a letter to Evans written towards the end of his time on the Itchen:

21st September, 1936.

Since I knocked off at the end of August the idea occurred to me, when tying some little Hassams,[1] to tie some as Variants, very lightly dressed, with hackles twice the length of the wing, and I have dressed a few accordingly for next year. But I told my friend Sir John Farmer about them and he dressed a couple, and writes about them as follows:

'I tried one at Castle Combe this afternoon. I was only able to be on the water for an hour and a half and caught five fish, two of them quite a good size for our little stream, one just over, the other just under, a pound, and the rest went back. But what impressed me was the *greediness* with which the trout rose to them—no hesitation about it. Every fish I placed a fly decently at took it *at once*. I certainly think they are a great discovery.'

Have you ever tried anything of the kind on the Usk? You might like to try the tip.

---

[1] By this he meant patterns representing the smaller duns tied after the manner of that great amateur trout fly-dresser, C. A. Hassam, whose work Skues greatly admired.

After this there is no further reference to Variants until six years later, when, writing from the Nadder Vale Hotel, he asked Evans for 'a few dark blue cocks [hackles] to tie Variants and Blue Uprights, sizes o, 1 and 2'. But we are not told what success they met with in his hands, or even whether he ever used them at all.

The method employed by Hassam for dressing his exquisite little split-wing duns was described by Skues in an article in the *Journal of the Flyfishers' Club*, which was subsequently reprinted in *Side-lines, Side-lights and Reflections*. Skues himself, after watching Hassam at work, adopted the same method of dressing duns, except that he used double-built wings (i.e. four strips of web all-told) in place of the single-built wings favoured by Hassam. This, however, was in accordance with precedent, for Hassam's flies were intended primarily for the limestone rivers of Derbyshire, where for centuries men have used lighter dressings than on the south country chalk streams. The reasons for this preference of Skues's is explained in a letter to Eastham.

30th June ,1943.

I cannot say that I ever used single wings except years ago in Derbyshire when I tried a local keeper's method of rolling a pad of starling or throstle with the shiny side outwards and using it in place of a pair of split wings. It did well enough there but I did not find it advantageous on the Itchen and returned to the split-winged floater. The trout seemed to be more attracted by a natural fly which fluttered than by one that was still. The rolled winged fly cocked all right.

My reason for preferring double to single wings for the Hassam type of fly is that the double wear so much better. One trout was about the limit on a single pair of wings. Hassam's single dressed wings were easier to tie and when new looked better, but once slimed in a trout's mouth the wings became tiny shreds.

In 1943, however, at the age of eighty-five, Skues evolved a fresh method of tying an upwinged dun and, with his usual thoroughness, had a brief description of it typed out to send to his fly-tying friends. In a letter to Evans he claimed for it the following advantages:

4th September, 1943.
The merits of the method are that it makes a very hard-wearing fly which sits up cocked and rides perkily over fast rippling water. A Scotch correspondent to whom I sent a sample pronounced it a winner.

The description, which was subsequently published in the *Journal of the Flyfishers' Club*, runs as follows:

1. Hook—Down-eyed, preferably Cleikum, o or oo.
2. Wax about one inch of one end of silk. Begin winding at middle of hook with waxed end of silk, so that by the time the silk has a firm grip the unwaxed part is reached, and wind to near the eye, leaving enough bare space for three turns of hackle and whip finish or two half hitches.
3. Take second or third or fourth primary of starling wing and straighten fibres near tip (excluding the dense part at the tip), so that they stand at right angles to the stem.
4. Tear off straightened parts and cut away root ends.
5. Divide material into two equal parts and lay one on top of the other.
6. With pliers double the material so that the shiny side is *inside* the fold.

7. Take the twice doubled feather in left hand fore-finger and thumb with tips to right and so that the middle of the fold is *upward* and the edges down-ward. This is important to get the wings rightly split.

8. Lay wing material with tips to right and whip two or three firm turns of silk and make half hitch in front of wings.

9. Lay stem of hackle along hook, best side away from you, and secure with three turns of silk.

10. Cut away roots of wing in taper.

11. Bring silk behind wings and whip to near tail.

12. Tie in whisks.

13. Spin on dubbing or tie in floss or quill and/or wire ribbing and wind to shoulder and secure.

14. Wind hackle three turns to right of wing and then one behind wing—four in all.

15. Wind silk through hackle back and front and secure on eye with whip finish or three half hitches.

16. Varnish finish and clear eye of hook and the fly is complete.

In his later years Skues also adopted a different method of tying his famous pattern of Little Red Sedge. This, too, he had typed out for his friends, but the essential difference between the new method and that described in *The Way of a Trout* is sufficiently clear from the following letter to Wauton. The Chaytor to whom Skues was indebted for the idea was one of the sons of the author of *Letters to a Salmon Fisher's Sons*, and the occasion referred to was a week-end on the Nadder:

30th August, 1938.

The only trout we caught in the two days were unsizable and Chaytor devoted himself to exter-minating grayling, which are innumerable, and on the second afternoon he got twenty-eight. . . .

Most of Chaytor's grayling, if not all, were taken on his variation of my Little Red Sedge. The wing instead of being rolled, as in my pattern, is split with the shiny side inwards. It has nothing like the lasting qualities of my version (I once visited the Chess with Dr Orton in August and with a rolled wing Red Sedge caught seventeen trout and five grayling and I gave the fly to Dr Orton who used it for the rest of the season) but it is a bit more quickly tied and the wings split automatically. He ties in the front hackle first *under* the hook then leaves a gap of about five turns of tying silk, then ties in the ribbing hackle, winds to the tail tying in the gold wire for the rib. Then he spins on the hare's ear for the body, winds the ribbing hackle to the tail and winds the gold wire through it (binding it down) and secures the wire just in front of the ribbing hackle. Then he straightens a width of landrail primary, tears it off and cuts away the waste ends, divides the feather into the two equal parts, lays one in the other and doubles them backward so as to expose the best side outwards, ties them down with three or four turns of silk in the gap, pulls back the front hackle and continues winding to near the eye, cuts away the waste and winds back to the wing. Then he winds the front hackle five or six turns, winds the silk through it and finishes with a whip finish or two half hitches at the head. A dressing of celluloid varnish at the head makes all secure.

Many amateur fly dressers, some of them complete strangers, used to write to Skues for advice on various points relating to fly-tying technique or materials, and he always did his best to supply the required information. The following are typical replies:

To Mr H. J. Smedley, of Derby, who asked for the name of the maker of the silk used for the body of Hassam's favourite fly and for the favour of a specimen hackle:

6th April, 1934.

Your letter of 4th instant has been forwarded to me from the Flyfishers' Club. I am sorry that the maker's name is torn off the only reel of amber silk I have, but a year or two before Hassam died he told me that it was no longer made in that shade and it is, therefore, unprocurable. I am sorry, as I should have liked to get another reel, not having many inches left.

I enclose one of Hassam's own hackles of the colour he used for the pattern which I described in the Flyfishers' Club Journal.

To Mr H. Andrews, of Saffron Walden, who wrote to consult him on a number of points:

6th February, 1946.

I have never but once had a lesson in fly dressing and have only my own amateur methods to rely on.

I cannot see why you cut up the fur for dubbing. You lose the entire advantage of the length of the fibres.[1]

---

[1] This refers to the hare's flax used for the body of the Gold-ribbed Hare's Ear.

I have used squirrel tail to *wing* a pattern of Sedge fly, adapting an American method, and it is quite a success. For dubbing bodies with squirrel use the back and *do not cut it up*.

Hare's ear and cow hair are both difficult but cutting them up makes them well nigh impossible.

I never mastered or indeed seriously tried tying in hackles by the point. *If you use good hackles* you can make a better job by tying in by the butt.

For spent spinners a hackle tied in by the stalk and wound and then bound right and left by figure of eight laps of the silk, the tips of the wings being humoured to shape, makes a good representation. For transparent wings I am content with a hackle of good quality, not tightly wound. I never cared for bundles of fibre tied upright.

The hare's ear pattern is very ancient. I am away from my books and cannot say how ancient. Like you I do not see the object of the red whisk. No doubt it does not look very red to the trout viewing it from below. Anyhow red does attract trout. The pattern Halford favoured in his early days had not gold wire but flat gold tinsel. No hackle but tips of fur from hare's face inserted between strands of tying silk and spun. To my mind that is still the best pattern both at the beginning and end of the season.

I do not use an oil bottle but have a pad of spongiopiline in a small box or a sovereign purse and saturate that with ordinary paraffin before starting and find it quite effective.

The term 'busking' I think hails from Scotland. I cannot give it any date.

To Eastham, who enquired which of several different methods of tying in a hackle he employed:

23rd March, 1943.

My practice is probably unorthodox and might be condemned by professional tyers. I have never liked and never preached the practice of tying in a hackle by the tip. I strongly suspect that it is used by professionals to enable them (1) to use poor hackles and (2) to use larger hackles than if they tied in by the stalk. Even in the poorest cocks' hackles the fibres are shortest and brightest at the tip. Amateurs who take pains to secure hackles of high quality can afford to tie in by the stalk. I always do. It secures the hackle more soundly and helps to taper the body of the fly.

For a hackled floater without wings I tie in at the eye with the stump towards the bend of the hook, winding over the stump halfway to the bend, then break off the stalk, wind to near the tail, tie in whisks, ribbing and quill (if any) at that point and in that order. I then wind tying silk back to foot of hackle, wind and secure quill[1] and then ribbing. I then wind the hackle backwards from the eye, wind the silk (held taut for the purpose) through the hackle (2 or 3 turns) and finish with whip finish or two or three half hitches at the eye. If there be dubbing I spin it on with the silk at the tail after tying in ribbing if any and wind it to the root of the hackle. I find that flies tied in my way are hard wearing and keep their shape.

[1] For 'quill' we should read 'body material', since Skues, as we have already seen, rarely used quill for the bodies of his flies and probably never for hackled floaters.

Although Skues's collection of fly-tying materials must have reached very considerable proportions in the course of years, he did not possess a cabinet but kept his main stock in an Elephant file and a ready-use supply in a wallet for ease of transport. These arrangements are described in a letter to the same correspondent, who had expressed interest in the wallet mentioned in the chapter on storage of materials in *Side-lines*:

November, 1942.

For a number of years I have kept a large supply of fly dressing materials at my fishing headquarters together with the necessary tools. The materials in a large Elephant file and the tools in a small bag with the silks, the wax and a small bottle of celluloid varnish, and I have only used the wallet to which you refer to amuse myself by tying a few flies on train journeys and on visits to other waters.

The wallet in question was not bought by me. It was the property of my Father's Father who fished the Don from Aberdeen in his youth and middle age, so the wallet may be for all I know a hundred years old. It is nothing but an old-fashioned fly book constructed to carry flies tied to gut in the usual compartments with a parchment addition which I got my women-kind to stitch for me. This consisted of three sheets of parchment sewn together at the edges, down the middle and across three times, dividing it into sixteen compartments with a round hole in the middle of each into which was tucked a small supply of dubbing, mole water rat, hare's ear, hare's poll, rabbit's poll (plain), rabbit's poll dyed hot orange, Tup's Indispensable material, English blue squirrel, opossum, black rabbit's blue belly fur, and a selection of seals' fur.

A small supply of the more useful hackles were placed in little packets tucked into the divisions constructed to take flies tied to gut. The pockets of which there were two held some peacock's herl and eyes, some floss silks wound on small cards, tying silks in skeins cut into lengths and threaded into channels in a silk container and other oddments. A leather band on the side of one of the pockets took scissors, pliers and old-fashioned hackle pliers until I replaced the latter with artery forceps which I kept in a waistcoat pocket with a tiny hand vice. If I wanted any other material the change presented no difficulty. At my fishing headquarters I had little occasion to resort to the wallet, as my Elephant file supplied all my needs. Wings when I wanted them on railway journeys I put in separate envelopes in my handbag.

It was, of course, a very makeshift arrangement, but it often served to while away a tedious hour on a railway journey.

When in 1945 Skues was compelled by advancing years to give up fly tying, he disposed of his more valuable materials, such as his collection of Hassam's hackles, to various friends. The remainder, still in the Elephant file, are now in the possession of the Flyfishers' Club, where the famous baby's plate in which he floated the products of his marrow-scoop autopsies does duty as an ashtray.

CHAPTER V

FISHING EXPERIENCES: ITCHEN

DURING his fifty-six years on the Abbots Barton water Skues had, of course, many interesting angling experiences. Most of these, however, have been recorded in his books, for it was his practice to illustrate the points he wished to make with tales of actual incidents by the waterside: this, indeed, is what makes him so eminently readable. Nevertheless, we are left with much in his correspondence which is of interest as showing his opinions on various matters connected with chalk stream fishing, and a selection of extracts from such letters is given in this and the succeeding chapter.

Although the Itchen seldom yields a really heavy trout, comparable to the heaviest from the Test and Kennet, the average weight on the Abbots Barton stretch was generally high, especially after the end of the 1914-18 war. It is therefore hardly surprising that Skues became somewhat fastidious in the matter of size and that it afforded him but little pleasure to catch 'small' fish. By this he meant trout of below 1½lb., which he returned to the water, and if he did not get a fair number of two-pounders during the season he would want to know the reason why. Thus when the size of the trout began to fall off in the 1930's, we find him complaining to his friend Wauton:

9th September, 1933.

After last week-end, 2nd and 3rd September, I knocked off trout fishing on the Itchen after the most disappointing season for years. It was not so much the number of trout taken that was disappointing, for up to the beginning of August and the hot weather I did pretty well, not infrequently getting my three brace limit; but the size of the fish was most unsatisfactory, as neither I nor any member or guest got a single two-pounder during the season, and I cannot recall even seeing a big fish from first to last, with one solitary exception, which was not seen again. The fish were in good condition and, as Evans would tell you, proved magnificent fighters—but I did want a few two-pounders. It made me feel that I ought to have pegged out at the end of the season of 1925 when I had ten brace of two-pounders, up to 3¼lb., with a number over 2½lb. The show of trout (1¼ to 1½lb. and over) which 1932 afforded made me expect a good run of fish from 1¾lb. to 2½lb. in 1933. I don't know whether the special fullness of the river had any say in the result. It is a fact that from the 1st April to the end of July I never saw the river without finding it over its banks. Weeds were also very heavy and that may have kept the big fish feeding below. We had no spring netting, so we had not the usual pointers (as to the stock we hold) we gain from that. There were exceptionally few trout in the side stream, but in August a pike of 8½lb. was wired down by the place in the park where we cross in the boat, and that may have intercepted many trout which would come up normally after the spring weed cutting.

A year later the story was much the same:

5th September, 1934.

It has been a disappointing season. Plenty of trout and they in magnificent fettle, but no rod, member or guest, has had a two-pounder. The shortage of water has not prevented the river from being bank full, for the mills have held up the water; but it has been dead slow. Moreover, in order to keep a head of water the weed cutting has been very light, and these two causes have altered the habits of the trout, especially in July and August, so that instead of lying under the banks for their fly food to be brought to them, they have been like lake fish and have cruised incalculably in search of their prey, and this has made them extremely difficult. The B.W.O. rise has not been strong, and when it has been the fish have cruised more exasperatingly than ever.

I am hoping to have one other season on the Itchen, but I expect next season will be my last. The past is my fifty-second on that water, and I turned seventy-six in August, and I am advised not to incur the fatigue of long days in the meadows. But if I have next season I hope that you will resume your old practice of giving me one week-end of your company.

Probably it was only his disappointment that led Skues to take this pessimistic view of the future: indeed, many of us at a much earlier age have felt inclined to give up fishing after an exceptionally poor season. At all events, Skues was to have eleven more fishing seasons after this, including four on the Itchen, and the reappearance of the bigger fish in the following year restored his equanimity.

Towards the end of July that year (1935) he landed a three-pounder, hooked in the tip of the nose, after a forty minutes' fight, and a week or so later he was able to report to Wauton:

6th August, 1935.

Bostock had five two-pounders last week-end down to midday on Monday, and may have added to them in the evening. I was broken three times by big fish and caught two of moderate size. I am told that there are some huge fish in the mill head at the bottom of the water and that they only come out at night. I am tempted to stay late and try a big sedge.

This happier state of affairs continued in 1936, when we find him writing to the same correspondent:

10th June, 1936.

It may interest you to know that after a series of lean years on the Itchen so far as two-pounders were concerned we had a fair number in 1935 and there has been rather a run of them this year—unfortunately coincident with a shortage of smaller stock, few fish under $1\frac{1}{2}$lb. being caught. Here is my little list:

2nd May	. . .	2lb. 5oz.; 2lb. 1oz.
16th May	. . .	2lb. 7$\frac{1}{2}$oz.
23rd May	. . .	2lb. 5oz.
24th May	. . .	2lb. 4oz.
29th May	. . .	2lb. 4oz.
30th May	. . .	2lb. 6oz.; 2lb. 8oz.
31st May	. . .	2lb. 8oz.
6th June	. . .	2lb. 9oz.; 2lb. 4oz.

They have been beautifully thick, solid, hard-fighting fish and only two have been taken on the floating fly.

He ended up the summer with ten brace of two-pounders, a feat he had only accomplished once before, in 1925. This is how he summed up the season to Struben:

24th October, 1936.

I am now nursing a broken muscle of my left leg, acquired through a bus pulling up with such suddenness as to throw me off my balance. I am only hoping it won't incapacitate me for 1937. This past season was my fifty-fourth on the length of the Itchen which you have fished with me. The season has been a peculiar one. For some wholly unexplained reason the grayling, which had become a nuisance, almost entirely disappeared (only one caught during the season). There were practically no small trout, scarcely any under 1½lb., and I got twenty from 2lb. to 2lb. 15oz., knocking off at the end of August.[1] A son of a member fishing late in September got one of 3lb. 4oz. on a Pheasant Tail in McCaskie's Corner, and a local angler fishing on the East side (among the cottages) with maggot got one of 4lb. 7oz. The conditions closely resemble those of the year after the War. The keepers had been called up and the pike had greatly increased. Result, no fish dared to lie out to take the fly unless he were too big for a medium-sized jack to tackle. We are netting shortly and may then find out whether my diagnosis be correct or not.

---

[1] In his later years Skues did not fish in September, maintaining that the trout were not then worth catching, and that too many of those caught were hen fish heavy with spawn.

Owing to the shortage of trout I found my colleagues viewing with disapproval my use of nymph patterns, and as I should hate to be fishing in a manner disagreeable to my colleagues, I gave up the use of nymph imitations about the middle of July, but as the trout continued taking under water I found I had to use sunk flies to get any fish at all. I finished the season on 29th August with a 2lb. 15oz. trout on a midge on a 0000 hook and 4x gut.

It must be admitted that Skues, in his old age, became difficult to please, for whereas in 1934 he had complained that, although there were plenty of trout in the water he had not killed a two-pounder, now that two-pounders were comparatively plentiful he began to grumble at the shortage of smaller fish. Thus to Wauton:

24th June, 1937.

You have not missed much (except an odd experience) in not coming to join me this year for a weekend at Winchester. Our stock of trout is deplorably low. I've only once known it lower and that was when we were eaten out by pike at the end of the War. Simonds professes to consider it is due to hard fishing, but I only killed forty-two trout (twenty of 2lb. and upwards and twenty-two of 1½lb. to 1lb. 15oz.) in 1936 and up to the present (in 1937) I have only killed seventeen—all but one of 1½lb. and upwards (including one of 2lb. 11oz. and one of 3lb. 5oz.) and the fact remains that this is the third year in which we have not had a genuine netting. In 1935 because of the drought when we had to leave the weeds to help to keep up the head of water and in 1936 because by reason of excess of water the stop net would not keep the bottom, and this year because the overflowing banks shedding the river at every few feet into the adjoining meadows made netting impossible.

Simonds installed a stew in a small side stream just above Mullins's hut from which 160 fish have been turned into the main, and about forty into the side stream, and sixty fish have been netted out of the Hyde brook and turned partly into the main and partly into the side stream. So at the beginning of the season we seemed to have in the upper water of the main below the railway bridge a number of small fish from ½lb. to about 1lb. 2oz., but it seems to me—I may be wrong—that they are scarcer now than they were—*I* have killed none—and again I suspect pike. Anyhow, we have had to enact a self-denying ordinance and abolish guests days, confining ourselves to sharing rods with guests.

What sizable fish there are (and I am speaking of fish of 1½lb. and upwards) are most confoundedly wary. For instance, on Saturday last young John Simonds was out with a guest all day. There was a nice hatch of fly and several fish feeding steadily in the bay below the boathouse. He was at them over an hour and I left them and went down to McCaskie's corner, caught and returned two fish of about 1¼lb. each and put down a third. When I got back to the bay and found that young Simonds and his guest had gone too far to return while the hatch of fly lasted, I found six fish rising pretty steadily on the far (East) edge of the bay, and after fishing them for nigh on two hours I fluked one—2lb. 1oz.—but could do nothing with the others, and that was the only fish caught that day.

Next day the bay was fished hard by Sir Gavin Simonds and his son and their guest all through the rise which last from 11 to 3, while Bostock and I stuck to another half-dozen fish at the bend below Rolts Stile, and though there was a lovely N.W. wind taking the line nicely across, not a fish could we take and the whole crowd went in 'toom'. Still, I would rather have them difficult like that than be catching a lot of stew-fed fish which is the expedient to which the minds of some of my colleagues seem to be turning.

The conditions appear to be exactly like they were after the War. In that case too, as in the present, the grayling which had been in great excess, practically disappeared. Yet then, when once the pike were reduced to manageable numbers and the big ones cleared out, the river recovered with great speed, and 1921 was a first-rate year, one of the best I have known. It is true that for three years we put in five hundred two-year olds of about eleven inches, but they went straight down-stream and in the March after they were turned in they were being caught in scores in the Town water by the locals on maggots, and after April they had totally disappeared, so that the recovery was not due to them but to the inherent quality of the water. I believe the same would happen again. The whole story of the war and post-war conditions is set out in 'An Itchen Retrospect' in *Side-Lines*. I daresay I shall not persuade my colleagues, in which case I feel inclined to put up my sub. in full for 1938 and resign, for I dislike the idea of fishing for stew bred and stew fed trout.

Most men would be far from dissatisfied with a season's bag of forty-two trout over 1½lb., nearly half of them 2lb. and upwards, fishing only at week-ends and knocking off in August. This, moreover, takes no account of the unspecified number of smaller fish returned to the water. But Skues kept no diary, and now, as he was nearing his eightieth year, his memory of earlier seasons may have become somewhat confused. Reference to 'An Itchen Retrospect' makes it clear that while in pre-1914 days bags were probably bigger, they declined in numbers when the individual trout increased in size after the war. Now he seems to have expected the best of both worlds. But in actual fact, in 1921, which he describes as one of the best years he had known, he caught by his own account no more than sixty-three trout, of which he kept only twenty, weighing forty-five pounds eleven ounces. Assuming that in 1936 he returned only half as many trout as he killed, the comparison is by no means unfavourable to the later year.

A month after this letter was written Skues got his record Itchen trout, which was duly reported to Wauton:

26th July, 1937.

I daresay you remember being smashed by a violent trout in the straight above McCaskie's corner. Well, on Saturday last, just opposite that spot, I hooked, on a nymph, a trout so strong that I had fought him down nearly to the corner before I even got him to my side of the river. At that point, however, he decided to go back, and that helped me by side strain to get him under my bank and eventually to net him out just above the upper hatch. He weighed 3lb. 14oz., a disappointment as the spring balance when I lifted him went down to 4lb. 2 or 3oz., but still the biggest trout by over half a pound I have ever had out of the Itchen.

It was also my twelfth two-pounder for the season.
Last season I had twenty, but there is no chance of
that for 1937. Still, the dozen included a fish of
3lb. 5oz., my biggest till then, and now this 3lb.
14oz. It being July I was fishing a 4x point, and had
to be jolly careful.

Once more his growing dissatisfaction appears in his
summing up of the season to Struben:

26th August, 1937.
My Itchen length has been behaving just as it
did at the end of the War when we were overrun
with pike. As then the grayling practically disappeared, no young trout worth counting coming
along, the rising fish few and big. Things are worse
than last year when I killed forty-two fish of $1\frac{1}{2}$lb.
and upwards. This year I have only killed twenty-
one fish of which twelve were two-pounders, including fish of 3lb. 5oz., 3lb. 14oz. and only one ($1\frac{1}{4}$lb.)
under $1\frac{1}{2}$lb.

Even so, his season's catch was one that many would
envy, and from his own evidence it is clear that he must
have caught and returned a number of trout below the
$1\frac{1}{2}$lb. mark. Presumably the solitary $1\frac{1}{4}$-pounder mentioned
above was badly hooked, for Skues never normally kept
fish of this weight.

No one has yet advanced a satisfactory explanation of
the phenomenon known to anglers as 'coming short': some
even deny the possibility of such a happening. Yet most
of us have experienced seasons when an abnormally high
proportion of fish risen have been either missed, pricked
or lost. Skues suffered this experience in 1933, as appears
from letters to his friends Evans and Wauton. To the
former he wrote at the beginning of June:

6th June, 1933.

The Itchen was very difficult during the week-end owing to the heat. On Saturday I got three fish, all of them pretty decent and all with a pale watery nymph tied with a white rubber body and a fine silver rib, and with luck I ought to have got my limit. The following day the fish were rising quite early and apparently pretty hard. I rose and missed three, all good fish, and got a brace, only one of which was sizable; all this before 11.30. After that I could do nothing with them.

On the Monday fish were again rising quite early and I left off at 1 o'clock with a solitary brace, having lost ten fish. I never knew them come unstuck with such desperate consistency.

And, two months later, to Wauton:

9th September, 1933.

Colonel Harding[1] was to have been my guest for my last week-end, but he was laid up with lumbago and lumbar rheumatism, and at the moment I heard of this from him I had a call from G. M. L. La Branche,[2] so I got him down instead. It was quite a nice week-end for weather, but I only got one trout and one grayling, and La Branche got one grayling, though he rose and held for a moment a trout of about 1½lb. on a huge variant with a greenish olive hackle. I could not imagine how he got such a fly to the trout as delicately and accurately as he did. I also hooked (and lost) a similar fish on a nymph;

[1] Author of *The Fly-Fisher and the Trout's Point of View*, a book of which Skues held a very high opinion.
[2] The well-known American angling author.

and I had a number of fish take my nymph and let go so quickly that I seemed nowhere near hooking them. This had been happening every week-end in August, when the natural flies taken (or rather their nymphs) were extremely small, but I am afraid my sight is going off, and that I am slower in the uptake. I suppose I must count on that, as I was seventy-five in August.

Characteristically, perhaps, Skues blamed himself for the failure to hook his fish, though it seems probable that it was not, in fact, his fault. At all events, although he continued fishing for another twelve seasons, we do not hear the same complaint from him again.

Evans also seems to have missed or lost a fish during a visit to Skues' water that same summer, which led to the following correspondence:

17th July, 1933.
You might be interested to know that on Saturday I got your fish opposite the stile. He took my pale watery nymph at the first chuck, with the merest hint of a wink under water, and he was not $2\frac{1}{2}$lb. or anything like it. He was an oldish cock fish not quite first-rate in condition, or he should have been just 2lb., being 16ins. long.

Skues evidently thought he had hurt his friend's feelings by this last remark and, characteristically, hastened to apologise:

19th July, 1933.
Many thanks for your letter of the 18th instant. I did not mean my comment on the size of the trout opposite the stile in bad part. I only meant it to

show how easy it is to miscalculate the size of a fish
that you only see in the water, and that none too
clearly.

To this the recipient added a note to the effect that the
fish in question was tucked in right under the far bank and
was a very deliberate mover.

From the letter dated 24th October, 1936, to Struben,
quoted on page 76, it is evident that some of Skues's fellow
rods were then beginning to view his use of the artificial
nymph with disfavour. This not unnaturally disturbed
him, not only because it led to a certain amount of friction
with his colleagues, but also because he believed that by
this time the long campaign he had waged to break down
the rigid dry-fly code, which had reigned supreme on the
chalk streams in his earlier days, had succeeded. Although
he was then in his seventy-ninth year, this led him to consider taking a rod on some other water, and at Christmas
time in the same year he poured out his troubles at some
length to his friend Evans:

28th December, 1936.

I see symptoms (one in the last number of the
Flyfishers' Club Journal) of a recrudescence of dry-
fly purism. I do not recall whether I told you in the
last year that I had one of our syndicate tackling me
on the subject of nymph fishing and objecting that it
was not fly fishing within the meaning of our agree-
ment with the landlord of our length of the Itchen,
and I found the other members of our little crowd
so much in sympathy with him that I agreed not to
fish nymph for the rest of the season, and had it not
been for the fact that, with our stock of trout so low
as it proved to be, it would have been difficult for
them to get a new member to replace me, I would

have resigned and looked for another rod elsewhere. As it is I have agreed not to resign for 1937 or, if I am still a going concern, for 1938. As it was I tried to get a rod on the joint Nadder and Wylye at Bemerton near Salisbury which my friend Dr Arthur Holmes used to fish and run, my object being to relieve the Itchen of my presence during Alder time and Mayfly time on the Bemerton length. But I failed to get the only vacancy as there was an old member who wished to return, and they naturally elected him. It seemed to make no impression at all on my colleagues that scarcely a single winged insect could be found in most of the Itchen trout taken.

But it is not for my personal problem that I want to secure your interest and help, but rather upon the general problem of the use of nymphs on chalk streams and elsewhere. C. E. Pain, who wrote a book called *Fifty Years on the Test*, told me that the nymph is now fished on the Test from Overton to the sea, and there can be no doubt that fishing with 'things called nymphs' has caught hold and is widely practised. If the nymphs used were genuine and fair representations of the natural nymph such as you and I use, there could be no case against it. But the case that I expect is going to be made, and with some truth, is that our practice is the thin end of the wedge, letting in the use of the innumerable abortions sold as nymphs. Two or three years back I gave a tackle dealer a series of my nymphs with specifications of their dressings, but within a month they were selling (and selling as mine) things which bore no least resemblance to my patterns and could not properly be called nymphs at all. Other firms sell nymphs of the Professor and the Bloody Butcher and a heap of monstrosities which look like beetles with whisks and bear no resemblance either in proportion, shape or colour to the natural nymph. . . .

The fact is the genuine nymph fisher is up against an almost invincible flood of ignorance on the part of the flyfishing public, who accept these abortions and monstrosities in good faith and no doubt catch trout with them now and again.

It seems to me that the best defence against this flood of abysmal ignorance and misconception is attack, and it is for this I would like to enlist your help. The difficulty is that the sporting press would probably decline to publish articles whole-heartedly attacking the productions of their advertisers. The most effective publicity, to my mind, would be a book on the use of the nymph, going bald-headed in favour of real representation. Do you feel inclined to come in? If I did it alone it would be put down to personal vanity. But independent support from such an angler as yourself would be much more effective. The book should have illustrations of good series of the nymphs and of good imitations, and should point out fearlessly how wrong most of the tackle dealers' stuff is. I hope you will consider this appeal and decide to come in on the right side. I am in my seventy-ninth year, and my energy is no longer inexhaustible.

Evans, however, felt that his own experience of nymph fishing on the chalk streams was too slight to justify him in taking an active part in a book of this kind and the project was shelved for the time being. At the Annual General Meeting of the Abbots Barton Syndicate in the following February, the members discreetly refrained from mentioning the subject of nymph fishing, but it was only a question of time before matters came to a head. Skues evidently realised this, for after the meeting he wrote to Evans:

8th February, 1937.

I expect my colleagues will be as averse to nymph fishing as they showed themselves last year. It is a pity. I wish they would read what Hills says about it in his new book, *My Sporting Life*, but it speaks so absurdly highly of me that for very shame I could not ask them to read it. It is all the more annoying in that at my age I have so little time still before me to pursue my studies of nymphs and their imitations. I *should* like to carry them a bit further. I have on occasion seen in summer evenings trout rising all over the water, making a funny little wriggling rise form, and on these occasions they seem uncatchable. I suspect nymph of *Caenis*, and I *would* like to try this out and to evolve a killing nymph pattern.

Skues's promise to abstain from nymph fishing was only given for the latter part of the 1936 season, and in 1937 he reverted to his favourite method, both the three-pounders already recorded being taken on the nymph. There is little in his correspondence during this summer to suggest further friction with his colleagues on this account, but the thought of the 'monstrosities' being sold in the shops as nymphs still rankled in his mind, and having failed to obtain the co-operation of Evans, he began to think of writing another book on his own. For a start, he sounded Wauton on the subject:

24th June, 1937.

I have been corresponding of late with a man who lives in N. Ireland and some years ago contributed to the *F.[ishing] G.[azette]* some highly intelligent articles on dressing and fishing with nymphs. He has latterly adopted my method of dressing nymphs and he wrote me the other day telling me how he gave three of my patterns to be tried out by a local angler on a water where a brace was about the average basket, and in one day he caught eleven good fish from 1lb. to 2½lb. and was broken twice.

But the tackle dealers, though many now profess to sell nymphs, will persist in foisting on to the public the most dreadful abortions and treat protests with amused, if stupid, contempt. I sometimes wonder whether if I wrote a small cheap volume devoted entirely to nymph dressing and nymph fishing it would do any good, but the forces of stupidity are amazingly strong and I doubt whether there be one flyfisher in a hundred who knows what a nymph is like.

Wauton encouraged him in this project, whereupon Skues at once set to work and by November he had completed the first draft, which he sent to Wauton for his comments and criticism. Curiously enough, he had never actually written a book before, his earlier volumes being collections of papers written at different times for the angling press, and he found the task more difficult than he had anticipated. However, aided by the wise advice of Wauton, he completed the final draft in the following year, and the result of his labours was published by A. & C. Black in 1939 under the title, *Nymph Fishing for Chalk Stream Trout.* For this, the final exposition of the art he had developed over so many years, we have cause to bless the tackle dealers whose sins aroused the wrath of Skues and prompted him to take action. Moreover, the scorn he poured on the so-called nymphs of the Bloody Butcher persuasion, coupled with photographs of actual nymphs taken from a trout's stomach and coloured reproductions of his own most recent series of imitations, had the desired effect. Doubtless the dealers themselves would have paid no more attention to his book than they had to his letters of protest, but by showing the nymph-fishing public what an artificial nymph should really look like, Skues created a demand which the Trade could hardly ignore. At all events, there has certainly been a very marked improvement in the commercial patterns of nymphs since the war, and if they do not all measure up to Skues's standards, most of them at least purport to represent actual insects, and the fancy names have disappeared from the catalogues.

In the meantime, a correspondence on the ethics of nymph fishing had been going on for some time in the *Journal of the Flyfishers' Club*, and this led to an organised debate on the subject in February, 1938. Skues, of course, took part and argued his case with his customary skill and logic, but it is evident that the weight of opinion was against him, and that, as he had feared, the old dry-fly purism was by no means dead. Whether this was the last straw that finally decided him to break with the Abbots Barton syndicate cannot be said; but at all events shortly after this he again entered into negotiations for a rod on the Nadder, and this time he was successful. It will be recalled, however, that he had promised not to relinquish his rod on the Itchen until the end of 1938, so he naturally made the most of his last season there. Scarcely had he laid aside his rod than, with feelings that may be imagined. he took up his pen to relate his experiences to his friend Wauton in a letter which, with the exception of a paragraph relating to fly dressing which has appeared in the previous chapter, shall be quoted in full:

30th August, 1938.

With the end of August I have finished my fifty-sixth and last season on the Itchen. I leave it with special regret inasmuch as, though I have not killed many fish, what I have killed have been a strenuous lot of admirable shape and fighting power and, with one exception of 1¼lb., have not been under 1½lb., and of those of 2lb. and upwards to 2lb. 14oz. (nine brace) half were 2½lb. and upwards. I have never had quite such a season where the two-pounders were more numerous than the fish between 1lb. and 2lb. Of course I did my best, generally successfully, to avoid catching fish under 1½lb. There have been several days entirely blank and in August the fish have been extraordinarily careful, those caught being hooked always in the extreme edge of the lip. One day I rose twenty-one fish and only hooked one soundly and he got off in the weeds. Of the fish I killed I almost universally took out the stomach contents with a marrow spoon and in most of them there was no single upwinged dun. I fished floating flies on the few occasions when I saw naturals being taken on the surface, but only killed two fish on floaters during the season. The rest took nymphs. The nymphs in the fish taken in July and August were extremely small. In the circumstances I do think that the purist attitude of my colleagues is a bit absurd.

There was one three-pounder caught during the season, 3lb. 8oz. by Bostock, the superbest trout I ever saw from any river but the Thames. It was only 1½ inches longer than a very lovely 2¼lb. trout caught the same evening on my rod by Chaytor who was

sharing it with me. Bostock had never used an Orange
Quill before, but took out a separate cast that evening with an O.Q. ready tied on and, failing to get
this fish up to T.[up's] I.[ndispensable] and other
flies put on the O.Q. and took him first chuck.
My sight has gone off of late years so much that I
have done no evening fishing, or my tale of two-
pounders might have been longer. But they have
been lovely fish.

I think I told you that, in order to have a water
to go to when the Itchen was no longer available,
I had secured a rod on the Nadder between Barford
St Martin and Wilton. I only visited it for three
week-ends. Once with Sir Grimwood Mears, once
with Barton and once with Chaytor. On the Barton
occasion I got a trout of 1lb. 14oz. on one morning
and two under the 12 inch limit. Barton tires easily
and I had to come in just as the Mayfly were beginning to come up a bit after half-past three. Chaytor
was down for the 18th and 19th June.

[Here follows the description of Chaytor's method of
tying the Little Red Sedge, quoted on page 65].

Chaytor drove me back on Sunday from Salisbury
to Winchester in his 30 h.p. Ford which is quite the
most comfortable car I ever rode in. He got fish of
2lb. 4oz. and 2lb. 5oz. in the two days during which
he shared my rod. [i.e. on the Itchen.] I also had two
two-pounders, one on a floater. I have had a number
of disappointments during the season, again and
again men I asked to share my rod being unable to
accept or failing at the last moment.

At the end of last year's season I expected that by the end of this, which would see me, if I lived, to eighty not out, I should be too old and tired to be good for another season, but, in spite of my four-score years I don't feel a mite less fit than I did at the end of 1937.

McCaskie[1] came down for one week-end to share my rod and became a convert to nymph fishing. It was a time in which the trout were feeding well and I had the exact pattern of nymph to please them. It is not always easy to find the precise pattern.

In spite of the gloom of my colleagues the stock in the water seems to be looking up. This length of the Itchen has always recovered from its sets back and it is justifying my prophecy that it would do so again. Thank goodness the grayling have disappeared, not one having been caught this season. I wish you could have come over and had a go at the two-pounders and had your line stripped off your reel in the first burst by some of them. Bostock had been having a week on the Test at Leckford lately and he says that, compared to our trout (not mine any longer, alas) the Test fish come in like pieces of string.

On one occasion this July I got a $2\frac{3}{4}$-pounder in McCaskie's Corner out of which among the nymphs I extracted one was alive, and not only alive but giving at intervals, in the cup of water into which I washed him, short convulsive wriggles propelling him not so much as half an inch and then resting inert for several seconds. Mosely won't have it that

---

[1] A great friend of Skues and owner of the 'Green Cat' described in *Sidelines*.

this is a fair illustration of the nymph's behaviour, assuming that it must have been damaged in the trout's inside. I think it must have been the last nymph the trout caught before my nymph caught him. Anyhow it was interesting. I never before (or since) found a nymph alive among the stomach contents of a trout.

During the month of August I found the fish sipping something incredibly minute and I found in the bellies of some trout which I caught some extremely tiny nymphs. I imagined that these might be in a youthful stage, but recently I have caught a couple of sub-imagines shaped like an ordinary dun but tinier than the *Caenis* and not so tubby, and they were two different colours, one very pale and the other a light blue dun. I never saw any mention of either in any anglers' entomology. Perhaps because they are inimitably small. I regret, however, not having had a shot on my tiniest Hassam hooks equal to oooo.

The publication of my Nymph volume is postponed to the Spring.

It is good to know that he ended up with such a successful season on the water he loved so well. And here, with him, we say Farewell to Itchen.

CHAPTER VI

FISHING EXPERIENCES: NADDER

In 1939 Skues, who was still working in London, spent his week-ends on the Nadder, which not unnaturally suffered considerably in his estimation by comparison with his beloved Itchen. In a letter to Struben he summed up his impressions of his first full season on the water.

19th December, 1939.

To make sure of having a water to go to [after leaving the Itchen] I took a rod on the Nadder for three years from April 1938 but I only fished it on two or three days in that year until September, and then I killed a lot of grayling[1] with which the water was infested. . . .

The Nadder, which runs into the Wiltshire Avon at Salisbury, is nothing like so good a river as the Itchen. There are a few biggish trout, 2lb. and upwards, very few medium fish, and none too many small ones coming on. I had trout over 2lb. of 2lb. 2oz., 2lb. 3oz., 2lb. 6oz., 2lb. 8oz. and 3lb. 3oz., and of medium fish only 1lb. 9oz., 1lb. 2oz. and 1lb. 14oz., in addition to a few about my personal limit of $1\frac{1}{4}$lb. Grayling were fewer than in 1938 and ran small. Best $1\frac{1}{4}$lb.

---

[1] No less than eighty in two weekends.

The Mayfly behaved most weirdly. It was hatching a few every day from 12th May to 1st September,
but I never saw one taken by a trout. My best trout
(bar one) were taken on Alder and Little Red Sedge.
The 3lb. 3oz. chap took an artificial shrimp in a
hatch hole. I imagine that, though I have to pay
my sub. for 1940, I shall see little or nothing of the
Nadder during 1940. I hope, however, to arrange
with my Landlord to give leave to Naval and Military men to fish without my accompanying them.
The rod entitles me to have a guest in my company
at any time.

I had by the way a little accident in the Nadder
water meadows in July. I put my foot into a concealed ditch and pitched forward on my face,
slightly dislocating something in my neck and I have
had a number of kneadings and wrenchings by an
Osteopath to get my head on straight again. I wish
I could say I thought he had been entirely successful.

To Wauton he wrote in much the same strain:

12th September, 1939.
The Nadder has been a great disappointment to
me. It contains, or contained, a few (very few)
biggish fish, not at all free risers, a very few medium
sized fish and apart from stock turned in this year
very few other trout at all. The wet Alder proved
(as experience of many years ago led me to expect)
as attractive as any pattern for the big fish. [Here
follow the details of his season's catch, as above.]

I took a fortnight off for Mayfly and never saw a
trout take a Mayfly. There was never a sufficient

hatch to hang the trout in, though every week-end from 12th May to the end of August there was never a day that I did not see at least one in the air, and on the 31st July I twice saw as many as five in the air simultaneously.

The hatch of small duns was pitifully small. They all seemed to be wee pale duns with greenish yellow bodies. I watched the webs carefully. Of a morning they were often full of *Caenis* spinners, mainly bright black, and only an occasional p.w.d.

The general direction of the stream is west to east so that the wind is nearly always down stream. Unfortunately when it is easterly there are few parts which are fishable by reason of trees and other obstructions.

I had to take a rod for three years when I joined in April 1938, so I have another year to run, but I imagine that, thanks to Hitler, I shall have to pay for nought. I knocked off at once when war was declared.

To Evans he gave a possible explanation of the scarcity of smaller fish:

18th September, 1939.

The reason why the Nadder holds so few small trout may be, I have been given to understand, that a previous lessee used this particular length for pike fishing with the result that the only trout that survived were the bigger old fish. Still those I have had of 2lb. and upwards have been in very nice order and no suggestion of the cannibal about them. I dare say the fact that there have been so many grayling has also something to do with it.

I omitted to explain that the Nadder, though it no doubt drains some of its water from the chalk, is not, like the Wylye and Avon, a pure chalk stream. The upper soil of the valley is very poor and when there is rain that is at all heavy the Nadder floods readily and becomes discoloured.

During the following summer, however, circumstances made him decide to retire from practice and take up his quarters on the banks of the Nadder. After settling in he wrote to his friend Wauton:

Nadder Vale Hotel, Wilton.   24th June, 1940.

Since I last wrote you things have been moving with me. On the 27th May a brother of mine, not the one you know, died after a long and wearing illness, and my eldest sister, who had kept house for me for many years, was too worn out with nursing him to be capable of carrying on. So I despatched her with two younger sisters to a safer spot than Croydon, shut up my house, giving notice to quit for Christmas, retired from practice on the 14th inst., and betook myself here, to remain till Hitler's attack has developed. If all goes well I must go back to Croydon for a sale of my furniture. If otherwise then to store it, if any remains to store. After that I hope to return here for the winter. You may remember that I have a rod on the Nadder, which runs at the foot of the hotel garden. There has been a long drought and the river is very low and acres of weeds show on the surface, uncut for want of labour. So the fishing is poor, trout being very scarce and grayling, mainly small, being a pest.

Most of Skues's correspondents, being a good many years younger than himself, were by this time too heavily involved in war duties to write more than an occasional letter. Consequently his own letters became much fewer in number at this period, and detailed accounts of his season's fishing are lacking. Nevertheless, he still continued to report his activities to Wauton from time to time. In a long and discursive letter written in July he described his visit to Winchester for the Eton match and his nostalgic reflections on seeing the Itchen once more:

7th July, 1940.

I went over last Friday week to Winchester to see my old school play Eton.

[There follows a detailed account of the journey and of the match itself.]

Next day I went up to revisit my old haunts on the Itchen and to shake hands with Mullins the keeper. It was a lovely day and a beautiful lot of trout were lying out, mostly under the far bank and sucking in nymphs voluptuously. It made me realise what I had given up. Bostock had been down the previous week and on the Thursday he had a peach of a trout 3lb. 6oz. It put my Nadder fish to shame. I do believe that these Itchen trout are quite the best quality trout in the country, though the Test trout go on taking the fly till later, four-pounders being not too uncommon. I have seen Itchen trout up to 4lb. 7oz. taken with maggot by locals, but for sheer beauty and hard-fighting quality the Itchen fish up to a shade over 3lb. are unbeatable. In my fifty-six years on the water I had twelve three-pounders, biggest 3lb. 14oz. I have seen several bigger fish, two I put down at 6lb., one at 5 and two or three at 4, but if they ever took a fly it must have been

exceptional. The Mayfly had gone since the beginning of the century or they might have taken that.
The Mayfly on the Nadder this year was a frost.
I never saw one taken by a trout and it did not, as
last year, dribble on long after it should have done.

The rest of the season seems to have been still worse, for
some six weeks later Skues wrote briefly:

18th August, 1940.
Winds here persistently down stream, rough and
gusty. Drought continues. Weeds uncut and river
dead low. I have had two trout in the past month
and even the grayling are not rising. One of the
trout the keeper told me was 4lb. and I got him in
ten minutes—1lb. 6oz.

Although now in his eighty-third year, Skues was still
able to stand up to a long day's fishing which might have
tired many a younger man. In writing to wish Wauton a
Happy New Year he concluded, with evident satisfaction:

30th December, 1940.
I had a day on the Nadder about three miles away
and was eight hours on my feet (10 a.m. to 6 p.m.)
in heavy rubbers, walking back, the last half mile
uphill, with my gear and 10lb. of grayling on my
back and was not a bit exhausted. So I feel justified
in hoping for one more season before I pack up my
rods, etc., for good.

The following year started better, though the river itself
was suffering from lack of attention. In July Skues wrote
a detailed account to Wauton with something like his old
enthusiasm:

12th July, 1941.

So far as I can see from the informal post-book I keep as a check, the 5th April was the date of my last letter to you, so you will have heard nothing of my Nadder results since. The season began on the 13th April with quite a strong rise of Grannom for one day and a sporadic appearance for several days after. My first trout was 2¼lb. Soon after C. E. Sykes, as my guest, got one of 2lb. 6oz. I had several others from 1½lb. to 2¼lb. before the Mayfly began to hatch. It was a week before the trout began to take them but in the week I had two of 2lb. 9oz. each and one of 2lb. 2oz. and was broken in weeds by a big fish on Iron Blue. Then on a Friday the trout came on to the Mayfly and I hooked 2 two-pounders, landing one 2¼lb. and losing the other at the net. In the afternoon of the same day in a stretch where I had only seen one trout rise this season I found six other risers and got another 2lb. 9oz. on Iron Blue. Next day I got another 2¼-pounder on the same stretch on Mayfly and lost another in weeds. Then the deluge came and next day the Nadder was a brown flood and when that had subsided all interest in the M.F. had departed. The weeds which had got a big start early burst into bloom on the surface and since then this length of the Nadder has been practically unfishable, being solid weed in most parts from bank to bank.

I am expecting McCaskie down on the 1st August for a week-end but I imagine he will get nothing but grayling. I have had one of near 2lb., one of 1½lb. and a few others of ½ to ¾lb. but nearly all have been small herring size.

The only places where one might hope for a trout are three weir pools but these are mostly occupied by bathers and the keeper can do nothing to stop them.

I had a funny set of experiences with a big trout, estimated at 3½lb, which in three days I hooked four times. I have set out the debacle in a paper for the *Journal* in which he is called 'The Imperturbable'. I will leave you to read the story there. It is not in the least exaggerated.

The lower Nadder, below Wilton Park, and the Wylye from Warminster to its junction with the Nadder below Wilton Park have been made a most horrid mess of by the Catchment Board which has dug out the bottom and heaped it in unsightly masses on the banks, spoiling all the flow and making the rivers look like unattractive canals, besides making them unapproachable for fishing in most parts. The Board, I am told, has been wanting to do this for years and has at length got military sanction. It may later, this year or next, come on up here on the same accursed errand.

And a fortnight later:

26th July, 1941.

Since I wrote to you for some unexplained reason the river has been v. low enabling me to wade to a nearly uncoverable spot adjoining a run about 2 yds wide out of a weir pool. Seeing a big splash in the run I waded across and offered a roughly dressed Spent Gnat. At the first cast up came a fish I have seen several times and put down at at least 4lb. and possibly 5lb. Alas I struck too soon and he would not come again. I tried next day, and within 10 yards of that run were three big fish (the 4-pounder, another about 3lb. and another 2½lb.) and a smaller one of 1½lb. or so. I fished them steadily from 5.30 to 8 and never put them down. They were not rising but were feeding hard under water. They would not look at the Spent Gnat and I tried several other flies in vain, eventually hooking the 1½ pounder on a red spinner, after I had made up my mind to go in. He kicked off easily.

Today there was no hatch of fly and though the 3-pounder was there I saw no other big trout and he stuck to the bottom. Sykes is coming on Tuesday to see what he can make of them. McCaskie is due on Friday the 8th August for the week-end and will probably have a try too if the weather is propitious.

I have been doing no evening fishing because my eyesight is no longer of much use in an owl's light, but the other day I saw that three trout had lined up between 6 and 7 quite close here. So next evening I took my rod and at sundown (about 9.40) I found a couple of risers and by 10 without moving from one spot had hooked and landed a grayling of about ¾lb. (a good fish for this water this year) and hooked and lost two trout. So I am tempted to try again when the weather is suitable. Not a sign of B.W.O. yet.

After the close of the trout season, Skues turned his attention to the grayling:

2nd November, 1941.

The trout season ended on the 30th September, my last trout being one of 2lb. 2oz. but since then

I have been operating on the grayling on the Bemerton length between Wilton and Salisbury and have had some tidy fish up to 2lb. 2oz., but the end of the season is in sight. It gets too cold and the days too short for me to carry on far into December. On top of that the Catchment Board, tearing out the river bed and piling it in unsightly mounds along the banks with slippery and dangerous slopes reduce the attraction for an angler of eighty-three.

The man from whom I have been renting my rod on the Wilton to Barford St Martin length is giving up his lease on the 1st Feb. and I don't know whether I shall be able to carry on, but I don't feel too feeble to try.

The unpleasant and seemingly unnecessary operations of the Catchment Board made Skues very angry, and from now onwards some reference to them appears in almost every letter. For some time past his correspondence with Evans had been very spasmodic, as the latter was too busy to reply, but in writing to wish him a Happy New Year Skues took the opportunity to give him his fishing news:

22nd December, 1941.

It might interest you to know that the Itchen syndicate fishing Winnal [i.e. the Abbots Barton water] gives up at the end of the year. They complain of insufficiency of stock (I doubt it, having seen lots of beautiful big trout when I went to see Eton v. Winchester in 1940 and paid a visit on the following Sunday) and that the cash is too much for three rods. . . . They might have put up a better reason than insufficient stock of trout viz. that a

Catchment Board for Itchen and Test is projected
and the landowners seem unable to resist it. To
quote the loss of fishing only puts a weapon in the
hands of the supporters of the measure who sneer at
sporting interests. For the life of me I cannot see
what good a Catchment Board could do in either
valley. In the fifty-six years I fished at Winnal
there were only two in which there was any excess
of water, and even the shallowest parts are seldom
less than 3 feet deep. I wish you could see what a
mess the Avon and Stour Catchment Board has
made of the Nadder between Wilton and Salisbury,
tearing out the bottom and piling stones in precipi-
tous banks often 10 ft. and more above the water
level and really reducing much of the length to
shallows.

My fishing landlord here has given up his lease
and the new owner has no vacancy to spare for me.
So I am reduced to membership of the club which
fishes the damaged stretch which gives me only
thirty days out of 153 in a trout season including in
the thirty days given to guests.

So, for the second time in his old age, poor Skues lost his
fishing, but although now in his eighty-fourth year he had
no intention of giving up the sport he loved as long as he
could wield a rod. He seems to have made quite a good
start to the 1942 season, which was duly reported to
Wauton:

14th May, 1942.
On Tuesday last with a rough and cold E.N.E.
wind we had the best hatch of duns, 1st, Large
Spring Olive and 2nd, Pale Watery, that I have

ever seen on the Nadder. I hooked eight, landed six and kept three—1lb. 9oz., 1lb. 3oz. and 1lb. The going along these stone-strewn banks is damnable. I had however only one fall as against three on a previous visit a week earlier, fortunately without breaking my rod.

During the summer he visited Winchester for the Eton match, as had been his custom for many years, and on the invitation of a member of his old syndicate had one more day's fishing at Winnal. This is how he described it:

2nd July, 1942.

I had a not wholly unpleasant time at Winchester for the Simondses were v. kind, but (1) Winchester quite deservedly lost the match (2) Not a soul of my day turned up (3) Nor did Sir Grimwood Mears (4) There were three herds in the meadows, each with a bull in attendance, so my fishing was restricted. (5) I only saw two rises all day though there was a strong hatch of little Pale Wateries on the main and the swifts, swallows and martins were having a hell of a time. (6) The river was full and dead slow being held up at the mills. (7) I rose one of the two risers and left the point of my hook in him and did not find out till I got back here. (8) My baggage went astray on my out journey and turned up three hours late at Winchester. On my return journey it was on the verge of being carried off from Salisbury to Bath when it was rescued by a porter I put on to the job.

From his final summary to Wauton, however, it appears that the 1942 season on the Nadder was very disappointing:

October, 1942.

Wednesday the 30th September ended the worst trout fishing season I have had for many years. All through the trout have been lamentably scarce, but on Monday I spotted a group of four bulging and hooked all four on a 000 Gold-ribbed Hare's Ear and lost all but the last (1lb 6oz.). I told a friend of your acquaintance, C. E. Sykes, who went down on Tuesday and reduced the remaining three by one. On Wednesday I went to the same spot and waited till about 12.30 for the trout to begin, catching in the interval three 14-inch grayling. Soon after 12.30 two trout began to bulge. I hooked and lost both. Their places were soon taken and I hooked and lost both the new arrivals, but by the time I had changed my fly another fish, this time a big one, had begun to bulge. Him too I hooked, I thought soundly at last. I had him on several minutes and got him out of four beds of weed only to lose him in a final irresistible rush. If I could have followed him down stream I might have saved him, but the banks have been made by the Catchment Board so steep and slippery and dangerous as to make that imposs. So the season ended with a disastrous day.

Even the grayling have gone off in numbers and size. One day I had a brace of $1\frac{3}{4}$lb. each, but nothing since over $1\frac{1}{4}$lb.

The 1943 season was even worse; so that, apart from complaints about the activities of the Catchment Board, there was little for Skues to write about. Indeed, the only mention of fishing is in two brief references to Eastham, with whom he had recently begun to correspond:

4th May, 1943.

Dr McCaskie and I were on the Nadder on the 1st and 2nd. On the 1st there was no fly till about 12.30. Then a lot of Hawthorn flies in the air. I had no pattern, never having seen them on the water before. Dr McC. had an imitation which gave him a brace. I only got one trout and one decent grayling and three herring-sized. Next day was bleak and rough and there was no hatch till 3.30 when there was a good lot of a small olive. Dr McC. got two grayling and put back one trout. I caught and returned five trout and killed five grayling before we knocked off at 4.45.

8th May, 1943.

I was on the Nadder yesterday and did not see a single trout rise from 11 to 4. The grayling did not rise to the natural fly till near 3, but I put on a Landrail Sedge on a No. 2 hook and cast to parts of the water I thought likely to hold grayling and before 12 o'clock I had hooked ten grayling and landed seven from ½lb. to a pound, all without moving thirty yards. It was tiring carrying them and I waited till 3 for trout to rise, but began fishing again about 3 when there was a hatch of fly and caught six or seven more, but had no offer from a trout nor did I see one rise. I saw one Mayfly.

His usual end-of-the-season summary to Wauton was much briefer than usual:

22nd October, 1943.

The past has been the most deplorable trout season I have ever known. Notwithstanding the prolonged drought the adjectival Catchment Board seems to have contrived to have every hatch opened whenever there is the least drop of rain, so that when one goes down hoping to find a little fuller river one finds it lower than ever. Their one idea seems to get every drop of water to the sea with the minimum of delay. The Wylye is in a dreadful state. The other day I walked ten paces perpendicular from the river bank on dry bed before reaching the water.

Though I *feel* well enough I must recognise that with the lapse of years I am definitely weaker. The other day in the water meadows I tripped on some loose barbed wire and fell heavily face downwards with face and hands in a bed of nettles and I found it quite a struggle to regain my feet.

Wauton, a much younger man, hastened to assure his friend that he himself knew what it was like to feel 'a bit weak on the pins', and that it was nothing to worry about, ending by advising him never to hurry. But it would have taken more than a tumble to keep Skues away from the riverside, and the following season saw him, in his eighty-sixth year, as keen as ever, though the death, in April, of his great friend Dr N. J. McCaskie came as a very severe blow to him.

Once again sport was poor, and Skues's letters to Eastham are full of complaints about the Catchment Board.

16th May, 1944.
The continued absence of rain is amazing. The Nadder is 2ft. below summer level as it used to be before the Catchment Board started its murderous career on it.

I have only been out three times so far. On the edge of eighty-six I find I tire too readily to fish a whole day. On the 5th May I found not a fish moving till 12 o'clock. Then without moving from one spot (about 20 yards) I got one trout 1¼lb. and sixteen grayling weight about 9lb. and then went in with all I could carry. On the 8th May I had a guest to whom I gave a black gnat (female) as I was going in with seven grayling (only two over herring size and those ¾lb. apiece) and he went on to catch on that pattern nine grayling weighing 11½lb. On the 11th I was at the top of the water and fished the racing water from fourteen hatches. I began at 10.30 and by 12.30 I had hooked nine trout, landed seven and killed a brace only of 1¼lb. and 1lb 10oz. The killing fly was like a No. 1 Whitchurch but tied with a hen blackbird wing. One of the returned I caught twice, on the second occasion recovering a fly I had left in him and a strand of gut. By 12.30 I was too tired to fish any more, though I stayed in the meadows till 3. It looks like my last year.

1st June, 1944.

The last day's fishing I had was on the 24th May. I began on the shallows below fourteen hatches but after over an hour's fishing I found nothing rising and walked down stream to the point where the Wylye joins the Nadder. Presently under the N. bank (I was on the S.) I saw one trout and then another and another till there were five, all of which I could cover without moving. There had been a lot of Alder about so I tried several with a small Alder, eventually hooking one trout and losing him in the heavy weed bed which broke the surface under my bank. There was a high bank behind me and the other trout took no notice and began to rise at a small pale insect. I remembered that on the Itchen, before the Mayfly died out, there was a two hours' interval between the morning MF hatch and the afternoon one during which the trout would take a small pale watery, and I put on one with a pale yellow silk body and pale ginger hackle and hooked a trout straight away. I got him ashore and put him back as under $1\frac{1}{4}$lb. Next cast I hooked one which was the biggest of the five I had seen and I was fortunate enough to get his chin on top of the edge of the weed bed and to net him (1lb. 13oz.). Soon after I hooked and lost another (which I did not regret as he was obviously under $1\frac{1}{4}$lb.) and a big grayling which came unstuck. Then I was tired and turned to go in, but at fourteen hatches I had a final cast and caught and returned a trout of about $\frac{3}{4}$lb. and packed up and went for my bus.

It must always be a difficult problem to decide when the time has come to give up one's favourite sport for good. The fisherman, however, has a longer innings than the followers of more strenuous pursuits, so that this particular problem is only likely to present itself to him if he lives considerably beyond what is normally considered Man's allotted span. Considering the apparently progressive deterioration of the Nadder and his own increasing physical weakness, Skues would probably have been well advised to lay aside his rod at the end of the 1944 season if not before, yet one can well understand his reluctance to do so while he was still able to throw a fly. In sending his customary New Year Greetings to Wauton he wrote:

1st January, 1945.

You will infer that I still cumber the ground notwithstanding my eighty-six years and the ground also cumbers me. I distinguished New Year eve by stepping on an icy bit of road and coming down bump on my stern, bruising myself for a handsbreadth from the tail upwards and am still rather stiff. My feet also are giving trouble as they did twenty or more years ago, but in the hope that it may yield to treatment and being unwilling to have such a deplorable fishing year as 1944 as my last I have subscribed for the Nadder for 1945 and hope to find the channel more perceptibly damp than it was in 1944.

But, alas for his hopes, 1945 proved an even worse season than the previous one, and although Skues reports the hooking of a trout 'near 3lb.' he failed to land one over the size limit, and at the end of the season he wrote to Wauton:

27th September, 1945.

You have often in the past made mock of my expectations of the end of my angling days, but now the breakdown of my feet and growing feebleness are making the 1945 season the end. . . . Rather tragic inasmuch as I have not in the seventeen visits I paid to the Nadder killed a trout, or hooked but one sizable one, or caught more than three grayling on any day and these herring size only. . . .

My hands have become so shaky as to render fly dressing a pretty hopeless job.

Eastham reminded him that Canon Greenwell (after whom the famous Greenwell's Glory was named) continued to fish for trout until his death at the age of ninety-seven, which drew the following reply:

1st January, 1946.

I knew that Canon Greenwell fished on to an old age, but I imagine his feet had not broken down and that he had not Catchment Board difficulties to contend with. I once read of an angler whose life ambition was to kill a 6olb. salmon. At the age of ninety he was still trying and was ultimately found dead on the river bank with a 6olb. salmon dead by his side—the perfect end.

And so, at the end of 1945 Skues gave up his rod on the Nadder, though for the next two seasons he often took his walks by the river, which ran close to his hotel, and enjoyed spotting fish and identifying flies. In 1948, however, the hotel was converted into flats, and at the age of ninety he was compelled, at length, to say farewell to the chalk streams for good.

CHAPTER VII

OVERSEAS CORRESPONDENCE

ONE of the most remarkable things about Skues's books, and even articles, was the way they attracted letters from fishermen in other lands. This is all the more surprising when it is remembered that his subject matter nearly always centred round the essentially English sport of chalk stream fishing. True, what he wrote was always both interesting and original, yet it seems that there was something in his personality which had the effect of making his readers want to take up their pens and write to him, even on the flimsiest of pretexts.

This, of course, was particularly true of Frenchmen and Americans, in whose countries the sport of fly fishing for trout has gained greater favour than in any other lands outside the Commonwealth. His earliest correspondence of this kind was with the famous American fisherman Theodore Gordon, and started towards the end of the last century when both men were contributing letters and articles to the *Fishing Gazette*. Gordon he never actually met, but a few years later his contributions to the light *v.* heavy rod controversy then raging in the columns of the same paper led to his making the acquaintance of W. D. Coggeshall, an American living in England, and the two soon became friends. In part II of *Side-lines* there appears a tribute to the memory of Coggeshall, reprinted from the *Journal of the Flyfishers' Club*, and another to the memory of a French friend, Louis Bouglé. It was chiefly due to the efforts of these three men that the first lightweight rods were brought across the Atlantic from America, thus forcing the hands of the English rod builders who, up to the first decade of the present century, had clung obstinately to the ounce-to-the-foot formula of the early Halford era.

Later still, when he had come to be more widely known through his books, Skues became acquainted with a number of American anglers, some of whom he invited to fish with him at Winchester when they were visiting England. A few of them, sponsored by Skues, ultimately became members of the Flyfishers' Club in London, and in return he was made an honorary life member of the New York Anglers' Club, thereby forging a friendly link between the two clubs which exists to this day. Skues, however, never recrossed the Atlantic after his initial voyage from Newfoundland at the age of three, so his activities as a member of the American club were confined to contributing articles to its *Bulletin*.

Amongst Skues's earlier American friends were three authors of angling books whose works are well known on this side of the Atlantic: E. R. Hewitt, G. M. L. La Branche, and the Rev. Henry Van Dyke. Unhappily his letters to these men are not available, but thanks to the kindness of the Secretary and some individual members of the New York Anglers' Club, a number of photostat copies of his later American letters have been received. Of these the following are a representative selection.

To Mr Richard Carley Hunt:

27th April, 1939.

It is extremely kind of you to send me the copy of Hewitt's *Nymph Fly Fishing*. I did not mean to cadge on you for a copy and I should like to pay for it, if you will allow me.

I see that his methods differ considerably from those which I have been pursuing for years on the Itchen and Test, and that the difference is due to the differences of your conditions. I see that Hewitt refers to the visit he paid to the Itchen some years ago when he fished it for two days as my guest. I think that my methods have progressed definitely since that date, and I have evolved a number of additional representations of the natural insect.

His book is a very interesting one and I notice that he seems inspired with a good deal of enthusiasm for the practice of nymph fishing. I shall be very pleased to inscribe copies of my books for you.

I imagine that by now you have been elected a member of the Flyfishers' Club. It is the practice of the F.F.C. for members to drop the formal 'Mr' and I would like to follow the practice with you, if you will agree.

To Mr L. K. Moreshead, Secretary of the New York Anglers' Club:

24th July, 1943.

I have lately found among my oddments two trout flies tied by the late distinguished American angler Theodore Gordon and sent by him to me in the course of our correspondence about the last decade of the 19th century. One is a Mayfly tied to gut with a cork body and Summer duck wings. The other is a small upwinged fly also dressed with Summer duck wings but with the fibres bunched in the modern manner. If the N.Y. Anglers would care to have them I will with pleasure post them to you or send them to any representative of the Club over here, as the Committee may determine.

And, on receipt of Mr Moreshead's reply (which, thanks to the war, did not arrive until nearly three months later):

14th October, 1943.

I am glad to learn that the N.Y.A. will accept the custody of Theodore Gordon's flies and have pleasure in sending them, hooked into the paper in which they reached me. Gordon's correspondence was a great pleasure to me and I greatly regretted his passing. He sent me a copy of the picture of him and his dog which was reproduced in the *Bulletin*.

The same post that brought your letter brought also the sad news of the death of another old friend George Benson Stewart whom I first met early in this century through my American friend Walter Durfee Coggeshall. Stewart was a first-rate fly fisher and we often fished together and tied flies together and he was associated with me in working out my earlier nymphal patterns and the method of dressing a nymph illustrated in the second coloured plate of *The Way of a Trout With a Fly* was suggested by him. He on several occasions fished the stretch of Upper Itchen fished by the late Viscount Grey (then Sir Edward Grey) and his friends and got consistently better baskets, mainly by the use of our nymphal patterns. He invented a most excellent little hand vice for fly dressing which I have often used in trains and his resource and ingenuity led me to picture him as 'The Novice' in a series of papers in the F.F.C. *Journal*, reprinted later in my third book, *Side-lines*. He was born in Canada but brought up in the States and after a period in Europe practised dentistry in London in Harley Street, retiring after being bombed out.

To Doctor Warren Coleman:

25th September, 1943.

The June No. of the Anglers' Club *Bulletin* reached me a few days ago and I am interested to see that your researches into the matter of Dame Juliana's dozen [flies] are dealt with in an article by S.G.H. and R.C.H. In October 1940 soon after my retirement my home in Croydon suffered a good deal from some bombing and I had to have my library packed up and deposited in storage where it is not easily accessible, so I have not been able to check the statements in the article as I should have liked to do and my memory at eighty-five is not as reliable as it was.

My impression is that Walton in his first Edition cribbed his fly dressing from Barker and in his second fell back not on the Dame but on Mascall who had cribbed from the Dame. You will no doubt be able to verify or correct this.

On the top of page 4 there is a reference to me in terms which are, I am sure, kindly meant but which I cordially dislike. To refer to me as 'the world-famous angling authority' is to expose me to the ridicule of those who know better. I have always objected to the term authority. See Foreword to *The Way of a Trout With a Fly.*

Apropos of Dr Lambert's reported remark to me ... I should like to quote a quite recent experience on the Wylye. A sharp rise began about noon but I could not find what the fish were taking and I tried five different patterns without getting an offer. I then tried a small dark nymph and had several false rises and hooked and lost one fish. Then I saw in the air an Iron Blue dun. I put one on and at once began to get some rises and hook fish and I landed five before the rise suddenly petered out. There may be times when any fly will kill, but my experience teaches me that it is well worth while to offer the fish the best possible simulation of the insect on which he is for the moment feeding.

To Mr C. O. v. Kienbusch:

1st March, 1947.

... As for the Pheasant tail, I have given all my fly dressing materials to the Flyfishers' Club, but I enclose two or three fragments left behind. They are from the appropriate part of a cock pheasant's tail. It is a Devonshire pattern and is quite a good fly, but not as magical as the 'British Angling Authorities' suggest. I have written out particulars of the dressing on a separate sheet so that you can have it typed out for our Club friends. Over here I should say it represents the male spinner of the B.W.O. Does not *The Way of a Trout With a Fly* contain a description of the dressing? I have parted with my last copy. In *The Way* it would not have been described as so general a fly.

The dressing of the Pheasant tail is, as Skues believed, given in *The Way of a Trout With a Fly*, but as the notes sent to Mr Kienbusch contain a few additional particulars they are given below for the benefit of fly dressers:

Pheasant Tail

This is a very attractive fly dressed in a number of sizes from No. 3 (=12) down to oo (=16) to represent a number of the rusty coloured spinners (imagines) of the Ephemeroptera. The dressing should be substantially as follows.

Hook. Size as above according to size of the natural fly.

Tying silk. Hot orange.

Hackle. Rusty or honey dun cock. (Sometimes a Rhode Island Red or even a ginger red makes a killing variation.)

Whisks. Same colour as hackle—stiff.

Body. Four, three or two strands of one of the three centre feathers of a cock pheasant's tail, tied in by points at tail.

Rib. Finest gold wire.

Specimen feathers for body enclosed. The strands should be tied in at the tail with tips towards the eye of the hook and wound evenly to the shoulder where they are secured by a turn or two of the tying silk and the waste cut away. Then the ribbing is wound to match the segmentation of the natural insect and secured. Then the hackle may be wound and the fly finished at the eye.

In November 1938 a young and ingenious American fly fisherman, Mr Baird C. Foster, wrote to ask Skues where he could obtain a marrow scoop, for the purpose of extracting the stomach contents of the trout he caught. This led to a regular correspondence between the two, lasting almost up to the date of Skues's death eleven years later. Extracts from the most interesting of these letters from Skues to Foster are given below, grouped together according to their subjects. The first contains a mild but characteristic rebuke:

24th November, 1938.

I do not know why you should have felt any hesitation about directing your enquiry to me. I imagine I do not differ from any other angler in being glad to put any information I have at the service of any brother angler. I may add that I am an Honorary Member of the New York Anglers' Club.

I am afraid, however, that you cannot be a very close or attentive reader or you would have seen on page 364 of *Side-lines* where the M[arrow] S[coop] is to be obtained. If you had addressed an application to the Army and Navy Stores, London, or even England, it would have reached its mark. The actual address is Victoria Street, London, S.W.2. The price has now risen by 3d. to 4/9d., but I dare say that will not choke you off.

The letter concludes with a description of the normal use of the marrow scoop for gastronomic purposes, which was apparently unknown to his correspondent, and thereafter the correspondence, thus begun, turned to the subject of nymphs and their imitations. Invited to criticise some nymph patterns enclosed in the next letter from Foster, Skues replied:

17th December, 1938.

I hesitate to criticise the dressings of patterns where I have no knowledge of the originals which they are intended to simulate.[1]

Our Blue-winged olive nymph is a flat-bellied crawler and if your *Ephemerella invaria* is of the same group I should expect it to conform more or less in

[1] Most species of Ephemeroptera of interest to American anglers are not found in England, and vice-versa: a fact of which Foster was possibly unaware at that time.

shape, in which case your pattern would be much too thin in the abdomen. In the next place the hackle strikes me as being rather on the long side.

If you have my third book, *Side-lines, Side-lights and Reflections*, you will have seen that I have abandoned the methods of nymph dressing described and illustrated in *The Way of a Trout* in favour of a simpler method.

The question whether the nymph will rival the dry fly in the U.S.A. depends largely on the relative extent to which your trout feed on the nymph near the surface. Over here waters, even on the same river, vary enormously. During the past season, of eighteen trout of 2lb. and upwards which I caught on the Itchen, sixteen took the nymph and only two the dry fly, and much the same proportions obtained among the fish from 1½lb. to 1lb. 15oz. which constituted the rest of my captures for 1938.

As regards your second pattern, again I do not know the natural nymph. My own patterns taper much more than your dressing and have much shorter whisks (about half the length). Your hackle, too, looks to me as if it would cause the nymph to float and is almost big enough to dress a spinner on a hook of the same size.

In the following February, Skues dressed some of his own nymph patterns which he sent to his new correspondent to illustrate his points, and a few weeks later he wrote:

7th March, 1939.

I am glad my nymphs pleased you. I am very fond of the pattern dressed with an abdomen of three strands of heron herl dyed in picric acid.[1] On its day it is deadly.

I don't like your idea of using caricature nymphs. For me much of the pleasure of fishing consists in taking the trout with representations of his natural food. So I don't care for fancy flies.

I have been reading Paul Needham's book which was sent me by Richard Carley Hunt, of the New York Anglers', and I should infer from that that you have more large insects than we have. Much of the charm of our chalk streams is in the small size of the majority of flies, so that the trout have to eat a lot to keep well nourished. Where there is a lot of large bottom food, the trout are poor risers.

In the meantime, however, a new and—to Skues—more exciting topic had arisen in the correspondence. Always ready, even in old age, to try out fresh ideas, he was greatly intrigued by some samples of the new du Pont material for casts which were sent to him by Foster. He passed them on to his friend Wauton, who was equally interested, and they asked Foster to obtain for them some casts and points for trial under actual fishing conditions. When these arrived Skues sent two strands to a member of the Flyfishers' Club, Major H. Nuttall, who had invented an ingenious machine for testing gut, but it was not until Skues took a fortnight's fishing holiday on the Nadder in June that he was able to try out for himself this new material, which he now came to know by the hitherto unheard-of name, Nylon. He hastened to report results to Foster:

13th June, 1939.

I found, during the past fortnight's experience of Nylon, three faults: (1) that the points are definitely

---

[1] This is his dressing of the Medium Olive for June and July, which subsequently became No. 6 of his final series of nymph patterns.

weaker than 4x gut; (2) that even with the points removed there is a tendency for flies to snap off in casting with a following wind; and (3) that the knots are difficult to tie and a bit slippery.

On the other hand, in sizes above the finest the strands are remarkably strong. I killed trout of 2½lb. and 2lb. 3oz. without a mark on the cast to show strain or abrasion by weeds or snags. I can see a good future for the material.

I sent an extract of your previous letter to my friend Major Nuttall, and I enclose a copy of his reply.[1]

Skues's interest in Nylon continued, and the subject frequently crops up in his letters to Foster after this. At the close of the next fishing season (1940) an unpremeditated test of a Nylon cast evidently pleased him very much:

2nd October, 1940.

I want to tell you of the performance of one of the Young du Pont Nylon casts which you sent me last year and I had left unused in an envelope till the 30th September, the last day of the trout season on the Nadder.

At the end of quite the worst trout season I have ever known I was coming in with only one small grayling as the result of my day. To get here I had to cross a latticed iron bridge on which I often put up or take down [my rod]. Under the upstream side of the bridge the farmer has put a wire (thickish iron), supported in the middle by a post, to prevent

---

[1] The gist of this was that the value of Nylon would depend on the strength of the knots into which it would tie, since knots reduce the strength of any material.

the cattle wading from the meadow below the bridge
to the better pastures in the meadow above. Against
the post and against the cement buttresses at each
end of the bridge cut weeds had accumulated on the
upstream side. I had taken off my cast, when something led me to look over the parapet on the upstream side and I saw quite a substantial trout just
above the wire and close to the left hand buttress's
accumulation of weeds. I had put away the cast I
had just removed and the first thing which came to
hand in my cast case was one of your Y[oung]
D[upont] casts tapered to .006. I tied on a grouse
hackled fly with a brownish yellow seal's fur body
and dibbed the fly on the water not in front of the
fish but behind and to the side upstream. It immediately began to take notice and came up to the
fly nearly touching it with its nose. I tried again
with the same result—and again. But the third time
after refusing it must have regretted the decision,
for it came up again and seized the fly. On feeling
the hook it promptly bolted downstream, under the
wire against which the cast was strained hard. I
dared not yield an inch expecting every moment to
be broken. But after my rod had been a hoop for
some time the fish bolted upstream and came down
on the other side of the central post and was once
more grinding the cast against the wire. Again I
held on like grim death and after a while feeling
resistance slacken I looked over and saw that I had
the trout's head out of water. But I had left my landing net out of reach at the spot where I stood to dib
for the fish and I had to manoeuvre the trout in
front of the pile of cut weeds collected against the

post to reach my landing net. This being safely
accomplished I reached down with the net through
the iron lattice work of the bridge and was just able
to dip out the trout. It scaled 2lb. 1oz. The extra-
ordinary thing, apart from the fact that the fish did
not break away, is that the cast shows no sign of
wear and tear from its friction against the wire,
lasting, as it did, several minutes.   ·

I wonder whether the Y.D. [Nylon] casts may
not improve with keeping. This was certainly
eighteen months old and may be older. Have you
any data on the subject?

This delightful letter, written with all his old boyish
zest, despite his eighty-two years, is in the best tradition of
Skues's books, in which he recounted many such incidents
to illustrate the points he wished to make. But as regards
the suggestion in his final paragraph, he was doomed to
disappointment, for in the following year we find this sad
sequel:

21st July, 1941.
The other day I used the 1939 Nylon cast on
which on the 30th September last I killed a 2lb. 1oz.
trout fishing from a bridge and having the cast
severely rubbed against a cattle wire without showing any signs of wear. I thought that that indicated
that Nylon improved with keeping, but alas it was
quite rotten and broke again and again. Perhaps the
strain it had undergone had taken the heart out of
it. I should be glad of your opinion.

Skues, as we have already seen, was always anxious to
encourage the breeding of fowls for their hackles, and he
was therefore delighted to hear that Foster kept Old

English Game birds for this purpose. Those parts of their correspondence on the subject which cover the same ground as the letters to Evans, quoted in Chapter IV, have been omitted from the following extracts so as to avoid repetition:

2nd August, 1939.

It is delightful to hear that you have been successful with Old English Blue Game. Several of my friends who have tried it have had unsatisfactory results. Often the feathers have had a bad taper, the fibres being short at butt and long at tip. A first-rate hackle should shew the fibres of equal length throughout so that if coaxed to right angles with the stalk for their entire length the tips form two parallel lines.

22nd August, 1939.

Thanks very much for your letter of the 14th and your interesting account of your dealing with your Old English Blue Game and samples you send. I return them so that you may understand my references.

I should call No. 1 a red. There is very little dun in it.

No. 2 is a great deal more gold than dun, though it has some dun in the centre. Its defect is that it is very chalky on the underside, which is not a common defect in the Old English Game as found in this country.

Sample No. 3 has quite a lot of life and spirit in it, but that again is rather chalky underneath.

Sample No. 4 is the best shaped of the samples you have sent me, and it is nice and springy. I don't like the white in the centre, or in one case in the root.

In the days when I kept fowls for hackles I didn't breed them especially for Old English Blue Game, and I managed to get some beautiful shapes and beautiful colours. . . . I have none of the hackles left for my own use, but I just kept a sample of one feather of each of the best birds, and I enclose you an envelope containing them so that you may see what my ideas of good hackles are; but I would like them back please at your leisure.

Your idea of breeding olive hackles amuses me. I hope that you will be successful, but I shall be astonished if you are.

29th September, 1939.

The specimen hackles I sent for your inspection are certainly not long in the fibre—that is one of their good points—and I should call the fibres very even in length if they were manipulated so as to lie at right angles to the stem. I consider that they take a lot of beating. It is difficult to find anything to approach them nowadays, in this country at any rate. You can return them as they were sent, by post, mentioning in the letter that they are returned so that it may not be supposed that they are an import.

Your scheme of breeding natural olive hackles intrigues my F.F.C. friends very much, but leaves them a bit incredulous. Of course, you have noticed that when you hold a red hackle of good quality to the light it does not look red but a bright greenish yellow. If you could eliminate the red without losing the greenish yellow sparkle something might be done.

The subject of fly-tying, of course, appears in many of the letters. In response to a request for the correct dressing of Tup's Indispensable, Skues wrote:

4th October, 1939.

With regard to the Tup patterns, I wish I had tied them for you when the weather was sunny and warm. Now it has turned so chilly that it is not easy to tie nicely and the tying silk is apt to break in waxing. But if I get a warm Sunday morning I will do my best to fill your bill.

I had the original pattern from R. S. Austin, the inventor, but I think I improved on it, and I believe he thought so too. His pattern was a red spinner only, and I developed the nymph and pale watery variations, besides some other patterns based on the same principle with orange, yellow and olive seal's fur replacing the red seal's fur of the original.

Skues's remarks on C. A. Hassam, the amateur fly-dresser whose technique he had always greatly admired and endeavoured to emulate, should be an encouragement to those who believe themselves to be too ham-handed to tie flies:

25th September, 1941.

Yes, Hassam was an exquisite fly-dresser. I endeavoured to describe his method in *Side-lines*. He however did not use a vice and with huge broad fingers and a thumb like a ham he turned out his little miracles in quantity on the tiniest hooks and delighted to give them away. I dare not use these tiny hooks on the Nadder. The grayling would spoil twenty or more for every trout they took.

Skues's views on translucency in the bodies of trout flies, and especially on J. W. Dunne's methods of achieving it, are of considerable interest:

3rd January, 1942.

J. W. Dunne I met before he published *Sunshine and the Dry Fly*. He was a friend of Dr N. J. McCaskie who introduced us. I had a correspondence with Dunne about his theories while his book was still on the stocks and I have his letters somewhere still. I had long been impressed with the value of translucency in trout flies. Indeed, in September 1888, a little more than a year after I had started fly-dressing, I tied two very effective patterns with bodies made of flat tawsy ends of gut strands (as one gets them in the hank) dyed a hot orange and wound over a bare hook shank. One pattern was a large red spinner, meant to suggest the imago of the August dun (a sort of pallid autumnal March Brown). The other was a tiny spinner tied with a similar body, a red hackle and wing of pale Jay secondary, to imitate an insect I caught in the air. The latter I only used once during that holiday (on the Coquet) but on the afternoon I used it I caught thirty-eight trout, using a single fly, while my companion, using three flies on his cast, one a red spinner, caught three. The other pattern took well at dusk, but oddly only if the wings were from the freckled part of the red feather from a partridge tail, that winged from the unspeckled part of the same red feather being quite unsuccessful. On the Itchen later I used a spinner tied with a body of similar gut dyed claret, also wound over a bare hook, with enough success to induce Halford to include it in the patterns illustrated in his *Dry Fly Entomology*. It is a curious fact that gut wound over a bare hook looks quite translucent and without any dark core of steel, whereas if it is wound over tying silk translucency is much reduced and the dark core becomes painfully visible. I did not however like the hardness of the gut bodies. Nor did my Itchen fish like them greatly, as I found I failed to hook them quite often when they rose.

It was not until the early twenties that I met Dunne. In the meanwhile I had tried other methods to achieve translucency, the most successful being the use of seal's fur for spinners. . . . I was impressed by his theory and got him down for a week-end at Winchester. He only got one trout (a two-pounder) and that was on his idea of a B.W.O. nymph. But I got his book when it came out, also a set of his silks and cellulite and I bought all his patterns except the Green Drakes. I never however could do any good with them, possibly because I hated the look of his cut hackles. McCaskie however did well with one of his patterns. But I still thought I could make something of Dunne's central idea of cellulite over a white enamelled hook, and disregarding his blending of cellulite I tied several flies with ordinary

K

starling wings and ordinary dyed olive hackles but with bodies of cellulite to my own fancy, and I found that when these flies came over a trout without drag they were generally taken at the first offer. But I also found that the cellulite cut and frayed and went fluffy with the least excuse, and that once it got fluffy it was of no attraction to the trout. The least touch of the serrated edge of a sedge ruined it as readily as did the teeth of a trout and one trout was fatal to the fly's future usefulness. These patterns took much longer to tie and were so readily ruined that I gave them up.

Skues, who always admired craftsmanship in any form, was intrigued to hear that Foster was an amateur rod builder. He himself had never attempted anything of this kind, but he held very strong views on rods and during his light rod campaign, with W. D. Coggeshall, he had gained a considerable knowledge of the subject. He himself, for many years, had used nothing but American-built rods, and Foster now wished to try his hand at copying one of these. He therefore wrote to ask Skues for the measurements, and received the following reply:

4th October, 1939.
I own two [Leonards] of the vintage period, a ten-footer of 1903 which I have not used for a number of years, and a nine-footer of 1905 which is my particular joy. Both are in three joints. I dislike the action of two-joint rods. They always seem to me to have a bone in the middle, spoiling the smoothness of the spring.

With regard to the measurements you ask of me, I imagine you won't care about the calibration of the ten-footer. The nine-footer is away at the moment having its whippings seen to for the second time in its thirty-four years' service. I have an engineer brother living with me who tells me that he has calipers capable of measuring to 64ths of an inch. But before I put him on to the job I would like you to tell me whether the measurements should be taken from angle to angle or from the centre of the flat of a side to the centre of the flat on the opposite side.

A discussion then ensued by post as to the best way of measuring the rod from which Skues, despite his lack of technical knowledge, emerged triumphant. But he never concealed his admiration for the skill of his correspondent in building a split-cane rod, and when at length the copy of his Leonard was completed to its maker's satisfaction, Skues lost no time in rejoicing with him:

26th May, 1941.

I am delighted to hear that your home-made rod built to the measurements of my pet Leonard promises to be such a success. If you get as much satisfaction out of it as I have had out of mine, since it was presented by a grateful client in 1905, you will be much to be congratulated. My friend Sir Grimwood Mears, who has shared it with me on the Itchen, calls it the World's best rod.

And again:

21st July, 1941.

It is also good news that the rod you made from the dimensions of my special pet Leonard has proved such a success. . . . I wouldn't take £50 for mine.

KX

Some years ago I sold the rods of a deceased friend in the interests of his widow and realised £52 5s. for the five—all Leonards—at 10 guineas apiece[1] less 5s. in one case for a damaged agate top ring. One of the buyers, on the first occasion he used it, was offered and refused £50 for it.

Later, he felt it advisable to give a few words of warning to the amateur rod-builder:

10th January, 1942.

While I am interested in your rod-making work and speculations I am wondering whether you are paying enough attention to the matters of hooking and holding. The late Major John Waller Hills (author of *A Summer on the Test* and other fishing books) fished with me as my guest several days on the Itchen and I noticed that though he cast a good line and rose fish he constantly scratched them only instead of hooking them. His rod was an expensive one of English make. There is an officer in the neighbourhood who bought a cheap split cane from a local dealer and it turned out to be a wonderful hooker and holder, though I doubt its wearing well. I have long been convinced that our rod-makers have little real knowledge of what in a rod makes it a good hooker and holder.

Then another very material point is the idiosyncrasy and temperament of the user of the rod. No two men are exactly alike and therefore the slight differences you notice between rods of the same

---

[1] This, of course, was before the Second World War, when prices were no more than half what they are now, and the very best English-made trout fly rod could be bought new for about £8.

make, same length and same weight may not from the practical point of view be so very regrettable, as they may suit a large variety of temperaments.

Foster, however, seems to have been quite satisfied on the first point, for a few months later we find Skues writing:

29th April, 1942.

Your rod-making abilities are most enviable. Do you find any difficulties with ferrules? Mills,[1] if I remember aright, told me that all their suction joints were made in Germany.

The hooking and holding qualities of your first home-made rod are remarkable.

Apropos of 'the even curve', I remember how my ignorance was sneered at in the *Fishing Gazette* when I spoke of it as an ideal.

I shall be interested to hear of your new design in fly rods when you are in a position to tell me.

Finally (though in fact the letter was written at an early stage of their correspondence) here is an account of a trivial but entertaining happening of the kind which Skues loved to retail in his letters:

2nd August, 1939.

I had rather an amusing incident on the Nadder two or three weeks ago. For some weekends a hatch hole with three gates with a strong current running through two of them had been the haunt of a biggish trout, and some smaller ones. The wind was persistently down stream all the time—too strong to

---

[1] The famous American firm who build the Leonard rods.

cast against. I had caught three of the smaller ones,
1lb. 3oz., 1lb. 12oz., and 2lb. 2oz. fishing down
stream, but the big trout would take nothing with a
drag. At last came a day when the wind, though
still down stream, was light enough to be cast into.
So I was able to tackle the big fish from below. I
tried several flies in vain, Alder, Sedge flies, nymphs,
etc., and then, as the only contents of the smaller
fish had been freshwater shrimp, I put on an imitation shrimp I had tied and had hold of him immediately. I was lucky in getting him ashore and
the landlord of my Inn weighed him (3lb. 3oz.). I
gave no directions when I brought him in, but next
morning I asked the keeper to take the fish up to a
farmer through whose land the water ran, with my
compliments. I heard no more till the Monday
when, as I was leaving to go back to my office in
Town on the conclusion of my week-end I asked the
Landlord's wife if she had acted on my message sent
through the keeper. She said she was very sorry but
that she and her husband thought they were at
liberty to do what they liked with the fish I brought
in[1] (which was true enough as regards trout of 1¼lb.
and under and grayling), so her husband had taken
it into Salisbury and sold it for 5s. 6d. I couldn't
help laughing and after that it was no good pre-
tending to be angry.

In May, 1947, a French angler, M. Paul Barbotin, while
on a visit to England chanced to see in the window of a
London tackle dealer a copy of *Nymph Fishing for Chalk
Stream Trout*. In days gone by he had read and enjoyed

---

[1] Like many trout fishermen, Skues did not eat the fish he caught.

Minor Tactics and *The Way of a Trout*, but the war had prevented him from acquiring either of Skues's two later books. He therefore pounced on *Nymph Fishing* with avidity, and as soon as he returned to his own country sat down and penned a long letter to its author, ranging over fly-dressing, entomology, rivers, and indeed nearly all those matters which fishermen never tire of discussing. Thus began what was probably the last 'pen friendship' of Skues's life, for he was then in his eighty-ninth year. In his reply he dealt in his usual methodical fashion with each point in turn, ending with the customary scolding to his correspondent for referring to him as 'an authority'. It seems, however, that M. Barbotin had assumed in Skues a greater knowledge of entomology than he actually possessed, or at all events of the scientific names of insects. For Skues had to confess his ignorance of the identity of *Telephorus lividus*, which Barbotin explained in his next letter is the common Soldier beetle. He also gave his own dressing of it, which he called 'Telephora', and enclosed a sample of this and two other patterns of his. Skues replied:

25th June, 1947.

Judging from your 'Telephora' pattern I am doubtful whether your natural insect is the same as our Soldier beetle. In July that swarms on the little thistle with the puce-coloured flower. The body is in two colours, half hot orange, half a pale yellow orange. To wing it I did not go to the expense of such wings as you use. The breast feather of the pheasant made quite a good imitation. V. killing.

It seems likely that on this occasion Skues was mistaken, for Barbotin's dressing bears a close resemblance to that of Leonard West, who, like him, used golden pheasant tippet feathers to represent the wing cases. *T. lividus* is, moreover, the correct scientific name of the English Soldier beetle.

Characteristically, however, Skues was not content to let the matter rest there, but followed it up with his usual thoroughness:

9th July, 1947.

I have sold or given away all my stock of trout flies that were any good, but I found among the experimental patterns I had left an attempt at *Telephorus lividus* which was incorrect in one particular. The body of our Soldier beetle is in two shades of orange, one pale the other bright, and I kept back the experimental pattern for a few days to see if I could catch a natural insect to show how the body colours should be divided. Normally at this season with the small thistle with the pale pinkish flower in bloom in the meadows just across the Nadder should be covered with the insect, but I think the bitter winds must have killed off the insect in an earlier stage for I have hunted the meadows for six days since the thistles were in bloom and have not found a single specimen. So I enclose my experimental pattern, which, but for the body being all hot orange instead of two shades, shows how I tied it for my friends and myself before my hands got too shaky—and a very successful pattern it was. You will note the cock pheasant breast feather for wing case. I think it more accurate than the far more expensive feather you use.

Now that age and infirmity had compelled Skues to give up fishing and fly-tying, he spent much of his time by the Nadder (where he was still living) observing fly life. A quest such as this—connected as it was with the sport he loved—was therefore no doubt very welcome to him and evidently put him on his mettle. One can picture him, within a month of his eighty-ninth birthday, systematically searching the water meadows for Soldier beetles, and at last his persistence was rewarded:

21st July, 1947.

I have been keeping a lookout for specimens of our Soldier beetle. Compared with previous years they have been few. I enclose a sample which may enable you to judge whether it is the same species as your *T. lividus*. The body of the artificial I sent in my last letter is too red. I should judge that to make an exact representation the dubbing of the body *when oiled or wet* should be the colour of a ripe carrot.

As many of Barbotin's letters consisted of questions and comments on a wide variety of subjects, Skues's replies are apt to appear disjointed, for it was his practice to number each point in his correspondent's letters, sometimes adding pencil notes in the margins, and then to deal with each item systematically in its turn. The following is typical:

10th July, 1947.

Your long and interesting letter of the 6th inst. reached me before I had posted mine to you enclosing an experimental but unsatisfactory dressing of the Soldier beetle, but I thought it better to post it in the hope that it might reach you before you left for your holiday in Brittany.

I wish I could supplement your stock of fly-dressing materials but having been driven in my old age and infirmity to give up fly-dressing as well as fly fishing, I gave all my stock contained in three large Elephant files to the Flyfishers' Club for the use of members. I agree that to buy feathers, unless you can make your own selection, is uneconomical and disappointing. It is not every hare that has a satisfactory poll in texture and colour. . . .

Your account of the black Leptophlebia reminds me that once in my early days at Winchester I found a large pale yellow Ephemera coupled with a shining black male. I never saw another example of either in the fifty-six years I fished the Itchen. . . .

The dressings of the March Brown are innumerable and I believe most of them are taken for Sedges. I do not understand your reference to Wickham's Fancy in this connection.

The Turkey Brown is a not uncommon fly on the Itchen, but I never saw one taken by a trout or found one in an autopsy. Ignorant anglers seeing the T.B. on a chalk stream assert that the March Brown occurs on chalk streams, which is quite untrue. I believe Canon Kingsley made the same mistake.

I never saw the Claret dun on the Itchen except in one year and then every bit of still water in my length had one or more floating dead on it.

I never observed the salient or spur on the July dun. My pattern proved very deadly in its season.

Of course trout have colour vision. The whole art of trout fly fishing is based on that fact. Your Kodak experiences (which I have not got) qualify you to discuss these questions in a way that is out of my power. Moreover I have only got one useful eye and that is none too good.

Curiously enough, what appears to have been Skues's record trout received no more than passing mention in his books, and then without giving the weight or stating that it was his best fish to date. But perhaps as it came from a German stream it hardly counted with him, for he recorded the weights of his Itchen trout with meticulous care. The following brief description of its capture is therefore of interest:

9th September, 1947.

In your letter of 30th August you referred to two sections of *The Way of a Trout With a Fly* namely 'A Borrowed Rod' and 'The Alder and Canon K.' I had recently sent to the *Salmon and Trout Magazine* a paper on the Canon's chalk stream flies as described in his *Chalk Stream Studies*, and to make sure that my new paper was not a repetition of or inconsistent with *The Way* paper I borrowed a copy of *The Way* and re-read 'The Alder and Canon K.' and was pleased to find that I needed neither to withdraw nor correct the new paper.

I took the opportunity to re-read 'A Borrowed Rod'. I found it told only of the *second* of two successive days on the Bavarian river I chose to call 'The Erlaubnitz' from the German word for leave, because in those days leave was easy to get. The previous day, using my 10ft. 6¾oz. Leonard and fishing between the same two trees that I could touch simultaneously with my two hands, I had killed on a Crosbie Alder the biggest trout I ever took (4lb. 6oz.). The Crosbie Alder was tied thus:

Hook. No. 3 sneck bend.
Tying silk. Crimson.

Hackle. Game hen, dark centre and ginger points.

Body. The tying silk well waxed and wound thick and covered with thin brown india-rubber, with tying silk rib.

Wings. Freckled pea-hen, a covert feather.

I was immensely pleased at getting that fish[1] from such an impossible stand, for I had to play him in a bit of river full of snags and decayed branches and my gut point was 3X. It was next day my holiday companion stepped on and smashed the middle joint of my 10ft. Leonard. Largely my fault for laying it down while he was about.

On hearing that Barbotin was unable to obtain jackdaw throat feathers (for the Iron Blue nymph) in France, Skues undertook to try to get some for him. The following letter refers to this and various other matters relating to fly tying:

1st October, 1947.

I have had no reply from my artist friend about the jackdaws.

The primary and secondary feathers of a woodcock's wing from a mature bird are quite firm and suitable for dressing Sedges.

The term honey dun is often used loosely. If I had not given my collection to the Flyfishers' Club I would have sent you some lovely h.d. hackles of my own. They had the woolly centre part blue dun and the edges a lovely yellow. The term is also used for a dun cock's hackle spangled with gold like filings.

---

[1] This is evidently the fish which is very briefly mentioned on page 213 of *Side-lines*.

Variants. A barrister of my acquaintance, now long dead, used two flies only on chalk streams (1) an Orange Quill tied as a Variant and (2) a dingy, nearly black, fly also tied as a Variant, and he was not unsuccessful, but I never took to them or even tied them. Nor have I ever used Dr Baigent's patterns.

Skues's memory seems to have been at fault here, for in two of the letters to his friend Evans, quoted in Chapter IV, he writes of tying Variants, though it is true that there is no evidence that he ever used them himself.

It looks as though, despite all the trouble taken by Skues, Barbotin never got his jackdaw feathers after all, for following is the last reference to them in the correspondence:

21st January, 1948.

This morning brought me a letter from my friend S. J. Lamorna Birch, R.A., whom I asked to get me a couple of cock jackdaws so that I might send you the throat hackles for Iron Blues. He writes that he has not used a gun for several years and latterly hardly leaves the studio, but he had asked three gunners to shoot him a couple. All promised faithfully, but so far never fulfilled. One even shot two on his roof but forgot to collect them. Birch promises to try again. I do not know the difference between the throat hackles of cock and hen jackdaw, but the North countryman from whom I had the pattern insists on 'cock'.

The remainder of the correspondence, which lasted right up to the time of Skues's death, turned chiefly on the question of a French translation of *Nymph Fishing for Chalk*

Stream Trout, which caused him a great deal of trouble and distress, owing to the misrepresentation of his ideas. Barbotin, whose knowledge of the finer points of fly-fishing and of the English language is evidently much greater than that of the translators, did what he could to rectify matters through the medium of the French angling press. So far as we are here concerned, this part of the correspondence is chiefly of interest as showing the correct definition of the term 'bulging', which has been the subject of much misunderstanding in the past, in England as well as in France. A single letter from the many in which the subject is discussed will suffice:

12th November, 1947.

On turning to *Parlons Mouche*[1] I found at page 99 in the chapter, 'Comment se porte l'adversaire', the following definition of 'bulging'.

'Quant elle happe entre deus eaux des larves en train de se transformer en duns ou subimago, c'est a dire de monter vers la surface pour y éclire.'

Now that is not the meaning of bulging as originally established. At an early point of the dry fly movement there were constant complaints in the angling press of the growing habit of the trout bulging when they were making rushes over weeds, the course of the rush being clearly obvious on the surface which was not broken until the trout having caught his nymph made a swirl as he turned to resume his post. 'Then', it was truly said, 'you might just as well throw your hat at the fish as a fly.' Now that is by no means the case when trout are feeding on nymphs on the way to hatch, for on such occasions trout were by no means so difficult. When

---

[1] A French angling book.

trout were bulging in the original sense it was
showed that there was seldom any noticeable hatch
of fly. On such occasions it was inferred that the
nymphs were migrating and not on their way to
hatch.

Latterly there has been a tendency, against which
I have protested strongly on more than one occasion,
to muddle up the occasions when trout are feeding
quietly under banks or in runs between weeds by
calling them bulging, but it is wrong. The author of
Parlons Mouche has no doubt been misled by ignorant
British writers on this point. I have known men, who
should have known better, guilty of the same error.
The term 'bulging' is not a very fortunate one, because a trout feeding quietly in a run under the bank
or between weeds and taking nymphs just below the
surface makes often a little hump on the surface
without breaking it. But if that is called a bulge the
other practice which I have described is left without
a name—and it needs one, *for it is not the same thing*.

It was shortly before this letter was written that Skues
and Barbotin met for the only time in their lives: a meeting
which proved both amusing and disappointing to the
Frenchman, who had been greatly looking forward to it.
On a visit to England, he writes, he and an English friend
arranged at very short notice to visit Skues (then in his
ninetieth year) at the Nadder Vale Hotel. On arrival they
found that Skues was out, but as he was expected at any
moment they decided to walk to meet him. This they
managed successfully (for as Barbotin says, the old man
was unmistakable), and turning back towards the hotel
began a conversation, which owing to Skues's deafness did
not progress very well.

After a few minutes, however, Skues said, 'I hope you will do me the favour of having tea with me at my inn', to which Barbotin's friend replied politely, 'We should not like to take up too much of your valuable time.' Whereupon Skues expressed his regrets, coupled with his pleasure at having met them, and to their utter consternation stepped into a 'bus which had stopped nearby and vanished from their sight—for ever!

CHAPTER IX

THE LAST CAST

In 1946 the new proprietors of *Game and Gun* who had
recently taken over that journal decided to make various
changes, including a change of name to the *Country Sports-
man*, to date from January, 1947. In order to give the new
venture a good send-off, the Editor determined to collect
the best possible team of writers for the first issue, and on
the fishing side his thoughts naturally turned at once to
the man who, by common consent, was the leading
angling author of his day: G. E. M. Skues. Yet it seemed
a good deal to expect one who already had four books to
his credit, had given up fishing, and had passed his eighty-
eighth birthday, to think up a fresh and original article at
comparatively short notice. Emboldened, however, by
their recent correspondence on the B.W.O. (*vide* Chapter
III), he tentatively broached the subject in a letter
addressed to the Nadder Vale Hotel, where Skues was still
living. He need not have worried, for within an astonish-
ingly short time there arrived on his desk the delightful
MS. which is reproduced below. Although it was not
written as a letter, it would be hard to find a more appropriate ending to this book.

At the beginning of the present century and
maybe for several of the last years of the nineteenth,
I contributed a good many articles, mainly on trout
flies and their dressings, to the *Fishing Gazette* over
the *nom de guerre* of 'Val Conson'. In those days the
Fishing Gazette had an American correspondent or
contributor named Theodore Gordon, who, though

he died comparatively young, lived long enough to establish a great name among American anglers and to have a standard American pattern of trout fly called after him; and our contributions to the *Fishing Gazette* led to a longish correspondence between him and me. Nearly every one of his numerous letters to me contained samples of American fly-dressing materials (feathers and dubbing mostly) some of which remain among the materials recently presented by me to the Flyfishers' Club. Among the feathers sent me were a few Summer duck feathers, the best of all in my opinion for winging Mayflies or for hackling Straddlebug patterns of that insect. My letters from Gordon, on my becoming an Hon. Member of the Anglers' Club of New York in 1927, I presented to that Club.

The fishing which has chiefly engaged my attention was a stretch of the Itchen, where the Mayfly died out about 1900. So it came about that I did very little Mayfly fishing for the rest of my life, and Theodore Gordon's Summer duck feathers remained unused until some years after I had retired from business in 1940, when I took a rod on the Bemerton Club length of the Nadder, where the Mayfly have the unusual habit of dribbling on through the trout season and on to mid-November. I amused myself during my leisure by tying two or three Straddlebug patterns with Summer duck feathers of Gordon's giving, but somehow I seldom used them on the Nadder and I had one specimen left after age and infirmity had led to my resigning my rod on the Nadder and giving up fly-fishing and fly-dressing for good.

It was after this that a kind friend sent me a ticket for a day on the Wylye, and said that if I did not feel equal to using it myself I might pass it on to a friend. A brother, some seventeen years my junior, was to visit me in July and was both able and willing to make use of the ticket. We drove together some two or three miles up the Wylye from Wilton and got on to the river on a day not far from August, at a place just above a mill, where, when the mill was not working, the surplus water was let off over a series of cement terraces into a small stream which joined the main channel below the mill. As we came to the tumbling water I thought I glimpsed a trout flash into the shelter of the white water at the foot of the fall.

We went down a few hundred yards to near the junction of the main stream with the let-off, and worked slowly and steadily up the let-off till we neared the terraces of tumbling water where my brother called a halt, complaining of fatigue aggravated by lumbago, and begged me to take his Leonard rod for a few minutes while he rested. I took off his fly, and, despite the lateness of the season —as I said, it was near August—I tied on the last of my Summer duck Straddlebugs. I picked the whitest patch of white water at the foot of the fall, and at the very first cast I thought I saw a dark body turn under the foam, and, raising the rod top, was at once attached to a trout, which my brother, refusing the rod, presently netted out. It was only 1lb. 13oz., but we did not see another trout rise all day, nor a single Mayfly either in the air or on the water. So I owed the very last trout of a long life, with over sixty years of fly fishing, to a correspondence of some fifty years ago with a kindly American, long since dead, whom I never met.

INDEX

Abbots Barton syndicate, 4, 86, 88, 102
— — water, 3, 4, 6, 7, 26n., 27, 30, 35, 71, 102
Aberdeen, 69
Alder, 108
— artificial, 48, 49, 94, 108, 134
— Crosbie, 139, 140
Aldermaston, 28
Alverstoke, 2
Angler's Entomology, An, 18, 21, 26
August (or Autumn) dun, 45
— — — artificial, 45
— — — spinner of, 46, 57, 128
— — — spinner of, artificial, 46, 57
Austin, R. S., 127
Avon R. (Wiltshire), 15, 16, 17, 93, 96
— (Devon), flies for, 47
Axe, R, 27, 28, 44

Baëtis bioculatus (binoculatus), 19n., 33
— *scambus,* 21
Baigent, Dr, 141
Barbotin, M. Paul, 134-144
Barford St Martin, 90
Barton, Dr E. A., 6, 7, 32, 90
Bavaria, 4, 139
Beckenham, 6
Bemerton, 84, 146
Birch, S. J. Lamorna, R.A., 141

Black gnat (artificial), 108
Blue Upright, 62
Blue-winged Olive (B.W.O.) dun, 18, 20, 36, 37, 39, 40, 73, 101
— — — dun, artificial, 31, 39, 40
— — — nymph, 119
— — — nymph, artificial, 129
— — — (or sherry) spinner, 37, 50, 117
— — — (or sherry) spinner, artificial, 31, 50
— — — rise, 16, 73
Body materials, 57-60
Bosnia, 4
Bostock, N. F., 31, 74, 78, 89, 90, 91, 97
Bouglé, Louis, 112
Brecon, 28
Brook and River Trouting, 41
Bulging, definition of, 142, 143

Caenis, 22-25, 34, 92
— artificial, 34
— *halterata,* 22
— *macrura,* 25
— nymph, 22, 23, 34, 86
— spinners, 95
Castle Combe, 61
Catchment Board(s), 7, 100-103, 105, 107, 111
Centroptilum luteolum (C.L.), 18, 19, 33

Needham, Paul, 121
Newbury, 28, 29
New York Anglers' Club, 113,
114, 115, 119, 121, 146
—————— *Bulletin* of, 11,
113, 115,
116
Norris, H. F., 44
Norway, 4, 29, 47, 48
Nuttall, Major H., 121, 122
Nylon, 121-124
*Nymph Fishing for Chalk Stream
Trout*, 9, 32, 87, 92, 134,
141, 142
Nymph fishing, prejudice
against, 5, 9, 76, 83-88
Nymph Fly Fishing, 113
Nymph, found alive in stom-
ach contents, 91, 92
Nymphs, American, 119-121
— monstrosities sold as,
85-88
— sponge, 43, 59, 60
— unorthodox patterns,
47, 48
— (See also under names
of flies.)

Old Barge, 2, 3
Olive dun with greenish
wings, 26
Olive nymphs, 41, 57, 121
and n.
Orange Quill, 36-39, 57, 90,
141
Orton, Dr, 65

Pain, C. E., 84
Pale Watery dun(s), 14, 17,
18, 20, 21, 95, 103, 104, 109
— — dun(s) artificial, 32,
33, 34, 109, 127
— — nymph, artificial,
81, 82
Pale Blue Quill, 31

Parlons Mouche, 142, 143
Partridge and Green, 27, 28
Pen-names of G. E. M.
Skues, 10, 11, 145
Pheasant Tail, 31, 44, 53, 75,
117, 118
Pictet, F. J., 20n., 26
Pike, 72, 75, 78, 80
Poultry breeding for hackles,
51-57, 124-126
Powell, James, 3
Procloëon rufulum, 17n.

Red Spinner, 57, 101, 127,
128
Reffitt, A Yorkshire angler,
41, 42, 44, 45
Rhithrogena haarupi nymph,
40n., 41, 42
— *semicolorata* nymphs,
43n., 58, 59
Roberts, S., 47
Romsey, 28, 29
Ronalds, Alfred, 20, 33, 46
Rusty dun, 53
— spinner, 31

Salisbury, 15, 84, 90, 93, 102,
103, 104, 134
Salmon and Trout Magazine, 11,
17, 18, 19, 32n., 139
Sawyer, F. E., 17 and n., 18,
19, 21, 25
Sedge-flies (Trichoptera), 27,
46, 140
— — artificial, 67, 134,
140
Senior, William, 3
Sennybridge, 28
Sherry Spinner, 50. (See also
under B.W.O.)
Shrimp, artificial, 134
*Side-lines, Side-lights and Reflec-
tions*, 9, 38, 62, 69, 78, 91n.,
112, 115, 119, 120, 127,
140n.